Advance praise for

The Joyful Child

"Warm, immediately practical, and fun, this book gives parents tools that can be used during the most stressful, chaotic parts of parenting. It reminds us that small, playful moments can create big, lasting change for building skills that help our kids thrive. If you thought mindfulness wasn't for you or your kids, get ready to change your mind, and watch tricky moments become much easier!"

—Tina Payne Bryson, PhD, *New York Times* bestselling co-author of *The Whole-Brain Child* and *No-Drama Discipline*

"Hope. This book brings simple hope that everything is going to be all right. A child's behavior is a signpost to their deeper needs, and this book shows you the pathway to understanding and meeting those needs. Kira Willey playfully prompts and encourages. There are no unrealistic expectations here, rather a feeling that someone is walking alongside you, telling you with quiet surety, 'You've got this.'"

—Kim John Payne, MEd, author of *Simplicity Parenting* and *The Soul of Discipline* and co-author of *Emotionally Resilient Tweens and Teens*

"Wow! Kira Willey has a special kind of magic. She takes profound concepts of child development and brain science and makes them instantly understandable and usable. Her great (and fast!) ideas for calming the chaos with children—with detailed scripts and adaptations—meet each individual child's way of living in the world. Best of all, she gets that children are wired to move their bodies, to respond to music, and to extend their mighty imaginations. If we meet children in those places, the result is joyful, mindful connection."

—Lawrence J. Cohen, PhD, author of *Playful Parenting*

By Kira Willey

Breathe Like a Bear

Peaceful Like a Panda

Mindfulness Moments for Kids:
Bunny Breaths

Mindfulness Moments for Kids:
Breathe Like a Bear

Mindfulness Moments for Kids:
Listen Like an Elephant

Mindfulness Moments for Kids:
Hot Cocoa Calm

Breathe Like a Bear:
First Day of School Worries

The Joyful Child

THE
Joyful
CHILD

Kira Willey

The Joyful Child

Calm the Chaos, Connect with Your Kids, and Create More Happiness in Your Daily Routines

RODALE
NEW YORK

Rodale Books
An imprint of Random House
A division of Penguin Random House LLC
1745 Broadway, New York, NY 10019
rodalebooks.com | randomhousebooks.com
penguinrandomhouse.com

A Rodale Trade Paperback Original

A note about QR codes: In scanning the QR codes in this book, you are acknowledging that you have read and agree to Kira Willey Productions LLC's Privacy Policy and Terms of Use and understand that Kira Willey Productions LLC collects certain categories of personal information for the purposes listed in that policy, discloses, sells, or shares certain personal information, and retains personal information in accordance with the policy. You can opt out of the sale or sharing of personal information anytime.

Art by Anni Betts
Arrow illustration: Accountanz/Adobe Stock

Library of Congress Cataloging-in-Publication Data
ISBN 9780593980606
Ebook ISBN 9780593980613

Printed in the United States of America

1st Printing

BOOK TEAM: Production editor: Loren Noveck • Managing editor: Allison Fox • Production manager: Mark Maguire • Proofreaders: Jennifer Abella, Andrea Gordon, and Dan Janeck

Book design by Ralph Fowler

The authorized representative in the EU for product safety and compliance is Penguin Random House Ireland, Morrison Chambers, 32 Nassau Street, Dublin D02 YH68, Ireland. https://eu-contact.penguin.ie

For Lola, Tristan, and Brody

Contents

Welcome to More Peaceful Days

WHEN I WAS EXPECTING my first child, all I really thought about was the tiny adorable outfits, that sweet baby smell, and humming lullabies as my little one fell peacefully asleep on my shoulder—I didn't get much further than that. Somehow I forgot my child would get older, have feelings, and be LOUD and sometimes annoying and contrary and get sick and not want to wear what I picked out for them.

Parenting young children is hard. There are so many days when everything goes sideways. I remember planning "perfect" days of playing at the park, nature walks, and picnicking with my three littles. Adorable! And then we didn't make it out the door for two and a half hours. The cereal spills, shoes go missing, and the youngest melts down because you cut their toast the wrong way.

As a mom of three, I've been there. I've weathered the full spectrum of parenting chaos, from toddler tantrums to picky eaters to won't-go-to-sleepers.

What I wish I had known then: with a slightly different mindset and a few small changes, my day-to-day experience of parenting could have been way more joyful. I wish I had put more of my attention and energy into small, mindful connections with my children during our daily routines, instead of worrying about what other shoppers would think of my child's oddly mismatched outfit or all the many, many other little things that don't really matter in the long run. There was so much I could've skipped obsessing over, and instead directed that energy into joyful connection with my kids.

Here's the great news: I can give you the benefit of my experience. I made all the mistakes first! (You're welcome.)

Looking back now, I wish I'd had even a basic understanding of how my children's brains worked. If only I had known how incorporating simple, kid-friendly, and fun mindful connection activities on a regular basis could have transformed my children's ability to calm themselves—not to mention strengthened our connection and brought more joy into our home. I'm not saying that it would have been all sunshine and rainbows, but it would have completely shifted so many difficult dynamics in our daily life for the better.

Back then, I needed help: real talk, relatable advice, and practical, doable strategies to help calm my chaotic days with my young children. I desperately wanted to feel less frustration and overwhelm—and more connection and joy.

Maybe you can relate. Maybe you picked up this book because you have a strong desire to feel more connected to your child. You love to see them lit up by the simple joys of moving their body, dancing and wiggling, singing songs, creating their own games. And maybe this doesn't happen as much as it should amid packed schedules, ever-present screens, and the constant rush of modern family life.

I'm guessing you want your child to truly experience the discovery and wonder of childhood before the real world and its challenges inevitably start knocking on the door.

Imagine for a moment: mornings where transitions happen smoothly, where a simple rhythm game or wake-up wiggle gets everyone laughing and focused, making it tons easier to get out the door. Imagine mealtimes becoming more enjoyable for everyone, including (and especially) you, and bedtimes where a playful breathing exercise helps your child settle down easily, without the usual resistance.

If it sounds too good to be true, I promise it's not. This is entirely possible, and I've spent the last two decades proving it.

I've made a career of my unique and joyful approach to mindful connection with children. Not only have I learned how to confidently help my own three children manage their bodies and emotions, but I regularly walk into rooms of hundreds of young schoolchildren and transform the environment from chaos to calm in a matter of seconds. (True—and I'll show you exactly how in the first chapter!)

The Joyful Alternative to Problem-Based Parenting

There are tons of parenting resources out there, and many contain genuinely helpful insights. The issue I have with a lot of "expert advice," though, is that it's problem-focused. These resources position themselves as the solution to what's broken—your child's behavior, your parenting approach, your family dynamic. This type of advice can inadvertently add to your mental load rather than lighten it, and that's the last thing we need.

You're already juggling school events, work deadlines, and meal planning, not to mention trying to remember when you last washed your hair. Do you really need one more expert telling you what's wrong with your family? The parenting advice industry thrives on making you feel inadequate: too strict, too lenient, too involved, not involved enough. It's exhausting, often contradictory, and doesn't account for your unique child and family.

I'm here to offer something different—a simpler, more joyful way forward. Here's what I propose: What if, instead of seeing parenting as an endless series of problems to solve, we approached our daily routines as opportunities to build an unshakable bond with our children that will support them throughout their lives? What if, instead of taking our cues from the never-ending stream of advice coming from "out there," we took our cues from the little humans right in front of us? Our children come with their own owner's manual—we just have to learn how to read it. They're telling us what they need through their behavior, their play, and their natural rhythms and tendencies.

Does your child love to sing, hum, and tap on every available surface?

That's a window into how their brain processes information—and how you can best connect with them through rhythm and music. Is your little one constantly in motion, climbing, jumping, and bouncing? That's valuable information about how movement helps their body feel good. Does your child get lost in building elaborate structures? They're showing you that focused creativity is the way they love to be engaged and learn.

These natural tendencies are your child's way of communicating how they best connect with the world, and with you. When you recognize and respond to their cues—by turning toothbrushing into a song or reading time into an active adventure with movement breaks—you're speaking their language. This kind of responsive connection builds a stronger bond between you, creating a secure foundation that makes literally everything else go more smoothly.

You know your child better than anyone else in the world. Despite what anyone suggests, your intuition about your own child is more valuable than any expert advice could ever be. We're parenting the children we have—the ones right in front of us—not the theoretical children in any book. When we shift from being overwhelmed by all the outside noise to listening to the wisdom that's already present, parenting becomes less about implementing someone else's system and more about attuning to the wonderful and complex little person you're already raising. This creates a parenting approach that's authentically yours, one that truly serves your child and suits your family.

Think of it like this: When most of our daily interactions with our children are of the herding-cats variety—managing the day, correcting behavior, or solving problems—we unintentionally miss opportunities for the kind of connection that makes them feel secure and understood. But when we proactively create moments of joyful connection throughout ordinary days, we're laying a foundation of security that makes our children better able to listen and pay attention, and more resilient and capable when challenges do come up.

This book is packed with practical tools: ones that turn everyday moments—car rides, bedtime, family dinner—into opportunities for mindful connection. They're not elaborate activities requiring special equipment or lots of preparation. They're simple, quick, playful practices that fit naturally into your day and speak directly to your child's innate way of experiencing the world.

Let me be clear: I'm not asking you to add more to your already full plate. We're all up to our eyeballs. I'm offering a different, more joyful way of approaching what you're already doing.

Why This Book, Why Now?

My journey with children's mindfulness, movement, and music began with my own kids, but it quickly grew into something much bigger. I've written seven bestselling children's mindfulness books that have resonated strongly with families worldwide—published in twenty-four languages and selling more than half a million copies to date. My children's mindfulness and yoga songs have been streamed more than fifty-one million times.

The overwhelming response to these resources tells me something important: parents and children everywhere are hungry for simple, playful approaches to finding calm and connection in our chaotic world. They don't want or need anything complicated or time-consuming—they want quick, fun practices that actually work in real life.

That's exactly what this book delivers. I've distilled my years of experience working with thousands of children into the most effective, accessible practices—the ones that consistently light kids up and bring meaningful change to families.

These aren't just cute activities (although lots of them are super cute). They're powerful tools grounded in how children's brains and bodies actually work. They're also incredibly practical—easy to fit into your real daily life with kids. And now, after years of creating resources directly for children, I've written this guide specifically for you, the grown-up who loves them.

So why write this book for parents when my children's books are already reaching so many families?

Because while my children's books provide wonderful, joyful connection activities that kids love, you need the complete picture. You as a parent need to understand why these practices work so powerfully, how to weave them seamlessly into your family's unique daily rhythms, and how to adapt them when life throws curveballs. Most important, you need guidance on your crucial role as the emotional anchor in your child's life—because your own state of mind influences everything in your home.

Think of my children's books as individual tools, and this book as the complete workshop—with instructions, context, troubleshooting guides, and a master plan for building a strong, beautiful bond with your child.

Here's my promise to you about this book:

- ✔ It's full of practical solutions and hopeful positivity—not parenting guilt or way-too-high standards. No doom and gloom here.
- ✔ Regardless of what you've been doing until now, you can start fresh today with your child. It's truly never too late for positive change.
- ✔ These tools are complementary to nearly any parenting philosophy. They play on every team.
- ✔ While the strategies are fully backed by research, I won't bury you in studies and data. There's just enough science—in plain language—to give you the "why" behind the practices.
- ✔ The first three chapters set the foundation in straightforward, simple terms.
- ✔ The following seven chapters deliver actionable tools: scripts, activities, links, and resources you can use immediately—as in right now.

Here's how I recommend you use this book: Read through the whole thing to get a complete picture of how mindful connection can transform your daily life with children, then use it as your go-to resource for whatever moment you're in—the chapters are organized around different daily activities, so you can jump straight to what you need. Want help with chaotic mornings? Flip to Rise and Shine. Struggling with mealtime? Turn to Time to Eat. Ready for a calmer bedtime? Head straight to Good Night. Keep it handy—on your kitchen counter or coffee table for easy reference. Think of it as your quick-grab toolkit for creating more connection and calm throughout your day, a resource you can come back to again and again when you need it.

Some of these practices might feel new or even a bit silly at first. Remember, you already know how to laugh and be playful with your child! These activities just tap into and build on the natural joy that's already there between you.

Start from a place of openness and give the practices a try. Choose what works for you and your child's temperament, and let go of the rest. Nothing is set in stone here—make the activities your own; they need to work for you and your family. Adapt them as needed to fit your unique child and circumstances.

And please don't even try to do everything that's in here or get it exactly perfect. It's about progress. Baby steps. Even learning a few new tools from this book will help you find a few more moments of joy and connection in your day. It will build on itself and grow, more than you can imagine.

Children are naturally joyful beings—it's their birthright, their default state. This book isn't about teaching joy or instilling it in your child; it's about creating the conditions for their innate happiness to flourish. When we connect with them on their terms through play, movement, and mindful presence, when we provide the space, connection, and understanding they need, we simply clear what's in the way.

The fact that you picked up this book shows how deeply you care about your child. I'm so glad you're here.

THE
Joyful
CHILD

A Joyful Way Forward

OUR CHILDREN are part of what many are calling "the anxious generation," a reference to Jonathan Haidt's thoroughly researched 2024 book, which offers compelling evidence for a mental health crisis among children. While Haidt's insights are valuable, they're also frankly terrifying for parents already doing their best in challenging times. It's true that children's mental health statistics are alarming, with anxiety, depression, and attention issues on the rise. Many parents, maybe including you, are understandably worried, searching for solutions and doing the best they can while carrying their own heavy burdens of stress and uncertainty.

Let's Change the Story

I want to shift this narrative. Operating out of fear helps no one. When we parent from a place of anxiety and worry, our children pick up on it. Our stress becomes their stress, our fears become their fears. This constant state of alarm doesn't lead to better parenting decisions—just the opposite: chronic stress actually narrows our perspective, causing us to make poorer decisions and to miss creative solutions.

Living in a state of parental panic doesn't protect our children; it only diminishes our joy in raising them day to day. Not to mention, it models anxiety and worry as default responses to life's challenges. No thanks.

What if, instead of an anxious generation, we could nurture a joyful one? I truly believe this is possible. When we approach parenting through the lens of joyful, mindful connection—honoring our children's natural tendencies and building their emotional resources through playful, present-moment engagement—we're not just helping our individual families, we're contributing to a larger shift in how children experience childhood.

Imagine children growing up able to regulate their emotions, focus their attention when needed, and maintain a sense of composure and steadiness even in challenging circumstances. Imagine them carrying these capabilities into adolescence and adulthood, approaching life's inevitable difficulties with resilience and optimism rather than anxiety and avoidance.

This vision is entirely doable. It begins with small, daily moments of connection in your home, but its effects ripple outward. Your (relatively) calm, regulated child influences their classroom environment. Your family's approach to challenges shifts how extended family and friends interact with their own children. Your lived example offers hope to other parents searching for a better way.

Here's What It Looks Like

My son was that kid. You know the one—while other three-year-olds happily sat in their grown-ups' laps during music class, mine was looping around the room, running in circles while I chased him, my face burning.

"Sit down," I'd stage-whisper through gritted teeth. "Look, everyone else is sitting! SIT DOWN." The teacher would give me that sympathetic smile that makes you feel worse; the other moms looked away politely as I wrestled my little tornado.

I tried all the things: threats, bribes, holding him tightly while he squirmed like an eel. I'd leave feeling defeated, wondering what was wrong with me, my kid, and why he couldn't just crisscross applesauce like everyone else.

Fast-forward nearly two decades. I've spent years figuring out how to meet kids exactly where they are—in their world of movement, imagination, and play. Instead of fighting their natural inclination to wiggle, dance, and explore, I discovered how to harness that energy to create joyful connection.

Compare that scene with my son to this one: I walk onstage in a school gym buzzing with fluorescent lights and packed with 350 kindergartners. They're incredibly wiggly and chatty, elbowing their neighbors; the noise level in the cavernous room is high. Teachers weave through the chaos, cajoling/commanding/yelling at the kids to be quiet and hold still.

I don't even say hello—I start to clap a steady beat. Instantly, curious children turn toward me; faces light up. I lead a simple, imitation-based rhythm and movement game, adding in long, deep breaths. In less than a minute, the room is quiet, the energy is focused, and all eyes are on me.

Magic? Nope.

Here's the difference between the first scene and the second one: In the first, I was fighting against my child's nature—trying to force him to be something he wasn't. (As a new-ish mom, success to me meant getting him to sit still, be quiet, and do what the teacher said.) What I didn't understand then was that my son wasn't being defiant or disrespectful. He was actually doing exactly what his developing brain and body needed him to do. While I was desperately trying to make him sit still, he was just trying to get the movement that helped him manage his body and emotions.

But at the assembly in the gym, I did the opposite. I started by tapping into children's natural love of movement and rhythm, then channeled that energy into focused attention. I didn't demand stillness; I invited engagement and created connection. The result? Those 350 kindergartners were more focused and attentive than my one little boy ever was in that music class—and it was (for sure) not because they were "better behaved." That had nothing to do with it. It was because I finally understood how children actually learn best.

Kids are hardwired for movement, play, and imagination. They come to life when we engage with them on their terms—they weren't made to sit still and not make a sound, or to listen to verbal instructions all day long. They're born to move, to clap, wiggle, and dance. To play games. To be silly and to have fun.

When we connect with children this way, two amazing things happen.

First, we find that we no longer need to repeat ourselves constantly, raise our voices, and plead for them to pay attention and listen. We're not going to battle stations about getting in the car or finding shoes, not to mention all the other tiny flashpoints that can totally hijack your basic Tuesday with a young child.

This shift can be nothing short of revolutionary. Imagine your stress levels coming way down as you stop feeling like a broken record stuck on an endless loop of "Please find your backpack." Your blood pressure isn't spiking every time you need to transition from one activity to another, expecting resistance. You're not battling that feeling of failing at this whole parenting thing because your child can hear the sound of a Twix wrapper from a mile away but somehow doesn't hear you call them to come sit at the table.

Instead, you become a much more calm, confident parent, easily able to navigate a grocery store trip with the kids without bribing, threatening, or leaving your cart in aisle five and making a run for it. You'll find yourself with way more energy for the things that actually matter, because you're not in a constant power struggle. The atmosphere at home will shift from chaotic battleground to (mostly) peaceful—and there will be a lot more laughter and fun.

And most important, you'll discover more joy in your relationship with your child as your time with them becomes less about managing everything and just getting through the day, and more about nurturing genuine, loving connection.

Here's the second awesome thing that happens when you consistently connect with your child in this way: they experience powerful positive changes both now and for years to come—immediate benefits you'll see right away, and long-term developmental ones that will serve them throughout life.

What You'll See Right Away

Your child will quickly begin to:

- Feel calmer in their body
- Pay attention more easily

- Handle their emotions better instead of melting down
- Expand their capacity for learning

Your child will experience the profound relief of being understood and engaged on their own terms. Instead of constantly hearing "Sit still," "Be quiet," "Pay attention!," they discover they can learn in ways that actually make sense to their wiggly, playful bodies. Their frustration level drops because they're developing age-appropriate skills to handle Big Feelings, instead of being bewildered and ambushed by their strong emotions until they inevitably explode.

Long-Term Benefits: Setting Them Up for Life

Over time, these small daily practices add up to major life skills that will serve them far beyond childhood. Your child will develop:

- Stronger executive function abilities: focusing, following directions, planning ahead
- A better ability to manage themselves without your constant intervention
- Greater self-awareness and emotional intelligence
- More empathy and compassion for themselves and others
- Healthy emotional habits that will serve them throughout their lives—from handling a playground spat to navigating complex relationships as adults

Bottom line: making these early childhood days run more smoothly is a total game changer, but you're also equipping your child with inner resources they'll carry with them as they grow, helping them move through the world with resilience, creativity, and genuine joy—both now and far into the future.

The Bonus: A Stronger Bond with Your Future Teen

There's an enormous bonus here that might not be immediately visible, but will become increasingly valuable: you're paving the way for a stronger relationship with your child into the tween and teen years and beyond. When you establish patterns of joyful connection when children are young, you create a foundation of trust and understanding that's crucial during adolescence.

So when the stakes get higher—your child faces peer pressure, complex and drama-filled social dynamics, and big life decisions—they'll already have a deeply ingrained sense that you're someone who truly sees and understands them.

If your kids are like mine, they'll still occasionally be surly and uncommunicative in their teen years, so you have that to look forward to. But this early investment in connection creates a relationship where your adolescent is much more likely to come to you with problems rather than hiding them, and to actually talk to you through the rough spots.

Ask parents of teenagers: they'll tell you that the connection they established with their kids when they were young becomes their most valuable parenting asset when hormones and high school enter the chat. By focusing on joyful, mindful connection now, you're not just easing today's challenges—you're making deposits in your long-term relationship account. Points in the bank that will pay off big-time.

Real Transformation Through Small Changes

It's a simple yet truly powerful approach. When you infuse just one or two of your daily interactions with positivity—turning a rushed morning routine into a playful Good Morning, Body! check-in (page 44) or a whiny car ride into a game of Outside Inside listening (page 69)—you're not just making that moment more pleasant for everyone. You're actually reshaping your child's brain in ways that promote lifelong emotional health and cognitive abilities.

And let's not overlook the fact that this shifts everything for you: your days become way more enjoyable too. Suddenly you're not just an unpaid Uber driver managing a series of mini-crises, doling out snacks while counting the hours until you can collapse on the couch. You're more present, calm, and centered, and there's a lot more joy to be had in your daily routines.

As any parent knows, when your kids are calmer and more connected to you, life flows better for everyone. The secret isn't in huge changes—it's in accumulating small, intentional moments within everyday routines you're already doing. No special training, no elaborate interventions. Just consistent, simple connections that turn ordinary days into easier, more joyful ones.

For example: Nearly every morning, Sherrese's daughter would wake up cranky. She hated getting dressed, and the daily time-to-get-clothes-on struggle left both mom and child near tears. "It was just how I thought the mornings were going to be with a preschooler," Sherrese said. "Then we started doing the Weather Report (page 46) each morning. Now we start the day by looking out the window to check the actual weather, then taking a deep breath and checking our 'inner weather.' She gets a chance to say she's feeling stormy, sunny, or cloudy, and somehow just letting her name it makes everything easier. It's such a simple thing, but it's honestly been a game changer for us. Now I can tell right away if she needs extra hugs or if we should skip the elaborate hairstyle that day."

Jin was frustrated by bedtime taking forever, as her anxious young son struggled with letting her go and getting to sleep. After trying The Worry Box (page 174) for a few days—her son would name his worries and put them in a special, imaginary box for Mom to "hold" overnight—his resistance to bedtime virtually disappeared. "He might say he's worried about Grandma, who's sick, or that his friend was mean at the playground. I tell him I'll hold on to those worries for the night, so he doesn't have to. And for the first time in months," she said, "he goes to sleep easily instead of calling me back to his room multiple times."

Early childhood teacher Lindsey says, "The 1-2-3 Clap! rhythm game (page 95) has helped transitions in my classroom so much! Before, trying to get twenty-five kindergartners to move from centers to circle time was total chaos. Now I start our quick clapping pattern with deep breaths between each round, and it's like someone flipped a switch in their brains. My co-teacher came in just as they were sitting down quietly and asked what my secret was! It takes literally thirty seconds, and works EVERY time."

These are tiny adjustments in a daily routine—a Weather Report game, an imaginary Worry Box, clapping during transitions. But that's exactly what makes them so powerful. There's no need to overhaul your entire parenting approach or invest hours of extra time. When children feel seen and heard, and are equipped with simple, child-friendly tools to manage their emotions, everything else starts falling into place.

In the next chapter, we'll look at exactly what I mean by joyful connection and how it actually works in the messy reality of day-to-day life with young children.

First, though, pause and take a deep breath. The fact that you're reading this book shows how deeply you care about your child's well-being—that commitment alone means you're on the right track. If you've been feeling overwhelmed or anxious about whether you're doing enough for your child, try to let some of that burden go. I promise you you're doing great. The path forward is simpler than you might think, and you already have everything you need to begin—your natural intuition, your openness to a new approach, and your love for your child.

Are you with me? Great. Let's keep going.

Presence Is the Path to Joy

I WAS SPRINTING THROUGH our usual morning routine while my son worked on building his elaborate block city in the other room. We were already running behind. As usual.

"Five more minutes!" I called from the kitchen. No response.

"Come on, time to get ready!" I called again, frustration building. Crickets.

"We're going to be late!" I called out louder, getting annoyed for real.

I could hear the blocks still clacking together. This was our daily dance—me giving increasingly urgent reminders while he remained completely absorbed in his world, oblivious to time.

Something made me pause. I put the peanut butter down, walked into the living room, and sat down on the rug near him.

"Tell me about what you're building," I said.

His face lit up. "It's Busytown! See this tall tower? It's where the mayor lives. And here's the fire station. . . ."

I listened for about a minute, then I said, "This is awesome. Will you tell me more about Busytown after school? I want to see how fast those police cars go over the bridge."

He looked at me and nodded, then hopped up and headed toward his shoes. "After school I'll build the bridge even better!"

That small moment—taking sixty seconds to step into his world instead of demanding he step into mine as soon as I called him—completely transformed our morning struggle. By the time we needed to leave, he was not only ready but excited about returning to his city later, chatting about his plans for it on the way to school.

This Is Powerful Stuff

With young children, these types of everyday moments sit squarely on the fence—they can unfold in completely different directions depending on how we show up. When we're distracted, rushing, or trying to do ten things at once, these moments can spiral into power struggles, leaving everyone feeling frustrated and disconnected. We all know how quickly that ship can go down.

But when we're truly present, physically and emotionally, what could have easily turned into a battle becomes a point of connection. Suddenly we're working together instead of against each other. The difference isn't the circumstance—it's the quality of our presence in it.

That morning taught me something big: simply coming into the same physical space, making eye contact, and connecting directly with my son made all the difference. Rather than trying to manage him from a distance, I created a bridge between his world and mine with the brief moment of genuine attention and interest. The rest of our morning routine flowed a lot more easily, with less resistance and more cooperation.

And the icing on this particular cake is that I felt SO much better about myself as a parent than I would have if I had continued to repeat the same instructions, voice rising each time, leaving us both feeling cranky and disconnected as we got into the car.

It Doesn't Have to Be Complicated

Let's get super clear on what I mean by "joyful connection" in this book, because it's a main ingredient in our special sauce, as you'll see in the next chapter. Throughout these pages, I use "connection" interchangeably with "mindfulness" and "presence." What they all mean is bringing your full awareness to what's happening—without judgment—and that includes being aware of yourself, your child, and the bond between you.

We tend to overcomplicate this concept of mindfulness; misconceptions abound about anything "mindful." Here's the deal: mindfulness is literally just paying attention, fully, to what is happening right now. The end.

Once we understand this, suddenly many everyday moments with our child can become mindful—and they can be kid-friendly, active, and delightfully fun. (In fact, these are the only kind I teach, because—let's be honest—if it's not enjoyable, your kids aren't going to bother, and neither are you.)

Mindful connection isn't a special technique or a certain parenting philosophy. It's just presence. Awareness. Being all the way here, right now, with ourselves and with our child.

The Science of Joy and Connection

I can hear you wondering: "Does this proactive approach really work? You're telling me it will actually create real change in my daily routines with my child AND positively affect their development?" Yes and yes. And science backs it up.

When children regularly participate in age-appropriate mindfulness practices—like the joyful connection activities throughout this book—neural pathways for self-regulation become stronger, attention improves, stress responses become less reactive, and emotional awareness develops more fully. One study of preschoolers found that just eight weeks of regular, playful mindful activities led to significant improvements in attention, self-regulation, and positive behaviors like sharing and helping others.

And here's why connecting with kids on their level (i.e., making it FUN) matters so much: positive emotions are also powerful brain-builders for young kids. There's honest-to-goodness research on this too, showing that children who experience more joy develop greater resilience and problem-solving abilities, and that positive emotions actually expand attention and enhance creativity. According to Dr. Dan Siegel and Tina Payne Bryson, co-authors of *The Whole-Brain Child,* back-and-forth moments of connection between parent and child literally construct neural pathways in a child's developing brain that support emotional regulation and cognitive development.

Translation: When your child experiences consistent mindful connection, their brain develops stronger self-regulation and attention skills. And when your child feels joy during everyday moments, their brain essentially becomes optimally wired for learning and emotional intelligence.

Um, yes, please.

You Might Have Doubts

Even though it sounds great in theory, you may be questioning how this translates to your actual daily life with kids. Let's talk about it. Here's what I often hear from parents:

"My child can't sit still, so this won't work for them." Well, you're right at home here. Neither can most children, especially mine—nor should they. The mindful, joyful connection activities in this book are specifically designed for wiggly, energetic, playful kids. Which means basically every kid. These activities involve movement, music, imagination, and play. We're working with children's natural tendencies, not against them.

"I don't meditate—too boring—and my child won't either." Good news: there's no meditation, boring or otherwise, in this book. No one's sitting cross-legged in silence and we're definitely not asking a four-year-old to "quiet their mind." The activities here are more like games—clapping rhythms, pretending to be animals, dancing, laughing, and moving. If your child likes to play (and they do), they'll love these activities. I think you might too.

"This is only for certain types of families." If you're thinking, "This sounds nice, but I'm not a hippie/yoga mom/laid-back parent," I want you to know: this approach is for every family. It doesn't matter if you don't buy organic, can't touch your toes, or lose your cool more often than you'd like to admit. These practices are for real families with real challenges.

"This is too religious/spiritual for our family." Mindfulness isn't religious—it's just paying attention to the present moment and noticing our thoughts, feelings, and surroundings. The practices in this book teach children fundamental awareness skills through simple present-moment connection, and they're entirely secular, based on child development, neuroscience, and effective parenting. That's it.

"I don't know anything about mindfulness." You don't need to. If you can breathe, if you can play, you can bring mindful, joyful connection into your home. The activities in this book require zero special equipment and no previous experience, and can be done in the ordinary moments of your day. I give you complete descriptions, actual scripts, and links to videos and songs. No special training required.

"I don't have time for one more thing." I hear you. That's why we're not adding more to your plate—we're transforming what's already on it. The approach in this book weaves connection into existing routines: morning wake-ups, car rides, mealtimes, getting ready for bed. You don't need to carve out an extra block of time.

"My kids have iPads, is that OK?" Yep. I'm not asking you to toss your tablets out the window and live like it's the olden days. Technology is part of modern family life, period. What the activities in this book offer isn't an alternative to screen time, but rather a complementary rhythm that helps ensure your child's digital life is balanced with essential human connection. The goal is to create small, consistent moments of mindful awareness that help children develop emotional skills no app can teach, while maintaining your sanity in this very digital world we actually live in.

"I have a special-needs child. Will this work for us?" The beauty of these practices lies in their adaptability and gentle approach, making them particularly valuable for children with special needs. These activities can be customized to meet your child exactly where they are. Their playful, movement-based nature respects different learning styles and abilities, allowing you to modify them to suit your child, and the short length prevents overwhelm.

All Parenting Styles Are Welcome Here

Maybe you're wondering if this fits with your parenting philosophy. Here's what I've learned: whatever your parenting style is, mindful connection complements it. It's neutral, like Switzerland.

If you're a structured parent who thrives on routine and clear expectations, these practices add flexibility and emotional connection without messing with the structure your family needs. You'll have tools to stick to your boundaries while building a stronger bond with your child.

If you're a free-range parent who believes in independence and natural consequences, these practices help you be more present and intentional. You'll be even better at showing up when your child really needs you, without hovering or taking over.

If you're a work-outside-the-home parent, these practices are designed for the reality of limited time with your child—and they prove that deep connection doesn't require long hours together. Many take less than a minute and can be integrated into transitions you're already navigating: getting your kids ready in the morning, coming home from work, dinnertime, bedtime. It's about the quality of presence, not the quantity of time.

If you're a stay-at-home or homeschooling parent spending lots of time on a daily basis with your children, these practices offer fresh ways to engage throughout the day. They help prevent burnout by creating moments of authentic connection amid the (let's say it, sometimes tedious) flow of daily life.

Practice Makes Progress

If there's one thing I want you to take from this chapter, it's this: joyful connection is a practice, not a "perfect." There's no final destination where you arrive, look around, and say, "We made it! We're done!"

This is a journey of small, mindful moments, repeated imperfectly but consistently. It's not about never losing your cool again or having children who don't melt down. It's gradually building a home environment where presence, awareness, and connection are the foundation rather than the exception.

When (not if) you get distracted, frustrated, or overwhelmed, just begin again. It's that simple. That moment of noticing—"Whoa, I'm really distracted and preoccupied right now"—is itself an act of being mindful. And each time you notice a disconnect with your child and actively work to repair it, you're not failing at mindful connection; you're actively practicing it.

This isn't about perfect parenting, believe me. I'd tell you the number of ways I've messed up as a parent, but we don't have that kind of time. But with the ability to quickly and mindfully connect with my children, having laid the foundation of trust and safety, I can make a genuine repair and move on.

What's especially beautiful about this approach is that it evolves alongside your child. The specific activities will change as they grow—what engages a three-year-old differs from what resonates with a seven-year-old—but the underlying principles remain. You're building a toolkit that can adapt and expand throughout your parenting journey, not a rigid system that your family will outgrow.

This Is What Matters

We've talked about bringing your full awareness to small moments of connection, but presence alone isn't the end goal. What you really want, and the reason I'm guessing you picked up this book, is to create more joyful days with your child.

When you're distracted, worried about tomorrow's meeting, or replaying this morning's argument in your head, you miss the smile your child is giving you right now, the funny way they're jumping into their pants, the small moments that, strung together, create a life. Joy lives in the present moment, and if you're not there to meet it, it might pass you by. Presence really is the path to joy.

What's Next

In the next chapter, I'm going to hand you a simple roadmap that will make this feel completely doable, even on your most chaotic days. (No more thinking, "This sounds great and all, but you don't know my life!")

You'll walk away with a clear, practical plan that you can use whether you're dealing with transition struggles, constant negotiations, lack of cooperation, or all of the above. This framework is going to become your new best friend—so effective that you'll see results immediately, and so joyful that both you and your child will quickly start looking forward to these moments together.

Ready? Let's dive in.

Here's Your How

Calm, Connect, Create

HERE'S A BOLD CLAIM, and I stand by it: nearly every aspect of family life you want to improve—from rushed mornings to bedtime resistance, to enjoying more moments with your kids instead of just getting through the days—can be transformed with three simple steps.

These steps create a positive feedback loop—the more you use them, the easier they become, and the more joy they bring to your daily life with your child. When you implement them consistently, you'll be amazed at how they transform even the most challenging family moments. This chapter shows you exactly how.

These concepts are so simple you might be tempted to dismiss them. Please don't! They're the foundation of raising a joyful child. Let's jump into each one.

1. Calm 2. Connect 3. Create

1. Calm

What This Means: Calm Yourself

What I'm talking about here, and maybe this isn't what you were expecting, is calming yourself. The single most important factor in raising a joyful child is—drumroll, please—your own state of mind. It's the parenting version of the oxygen mask thing on the plane.

I know, it's not what you wanted to hear. Maybe you're thinking: "Isn't there something easier? A pill I can take, maybe? Do I really have to feel my feelings, and then deal with them?"

Here's the truth: children are emotional sponges. They absorb our energy—whether that's calm or chaos—and reflect it right back to us. The research on this is crystal clear: teachers' self-reported burnout directly correlates with higher stress hormone levels in their students, as measured by medical tests. Your emotional state—whatever it is, from super-stressed to Buddha-calm—is contagious. Full stop.

Our Energy Sets the Tone

When my daughter was about four, she went through a phase of epic morning meltdowns—the kind where getting dressed involved tears, negotiations, and massive aggravation for both of us.

One particularly rough morning, after trying every trick in the book I had at the time (reasoning, pleading, threats), I felt my frustration boiling over. I was about to lose my marbles completely when my phone rang. It was a work call I had to take.

In an instant, my voice transformed from exasperated mom to cool-and-collected professional. "Oh, hi! Yes, so nice to hear from you!" I said cheerily, stepping into the hallway.

When I returned three minutes later, my daughter was calmly putting on her tights. No drama, just a little girl getting dressed like it was the most normal thing in the world. Which in our house, it was definitely not.

I stood there, relieved but honestly baffled. And then I realized the only thing that had changed about the situation: my energy. When I shifted from frustrated to calm, she shifted too. Talk about a wake-up call.

I'm not saying you have to be zen all the time (impossible) or that you can't have human emotions (also impossible). I'm saying that your ability to remain relatively calm during chaos is the foundation for everything else.

Throughout this book, you'll find Calm Starts with You strategies specifically designed to help you find your center when things around you feel rushed, messy, tedious, or are spinning out of control. Use them. Practice them. They're not for your child—they're for you. But here's the critical thing: when you care for your own emotional state, your child benefits too.

Remember that children learn way more from what we do than what we say. If we command them to take deep breaths while we're visibly stressed, our actions speak a whole lot louder than our words. But when they see us actively practicing the tools we're teaching—breathing through frustration, taking a moment to reset—they internalize those skills in a way that no lecture could ever achieve. Calming yourself first isn't selfish; it's strategic.

To help support you, you'll find "Mama Mantras" sprinkled throughout this book—simple phrases you can repeat to yourself when things get overwhelming. (They work beautifully for dads, grandparents, and teachers too!)

What This Also Means: Calm Your Environment

This means looking at your family's rhythm and environment with fresh eyes. Are you rushing from activity to activity? Is your schedule so packed that there's no breathing room? Does your physical space feel chaotic or busy, with screens on too much and clutter lying about? One of the most powerful things we can do is calm our space—literally and figuratively—which lays the foundation for everything else to work more smoothly.

In the Setting the Stage sections in the following chapters, you'll find simple, doable ways to lay this calm foundation. Creating a home environment that feels peaceful and supportive doesn't mean a complete lifestyle overhaul—I'm not asking you to grab garbage bags and Marie Kondo your whole house—just small, intentional shifts that make a huge difference in how your family moves through the day.

What This Doesn't Mean: Calm Your Child

Let me be clear about what "calm" in this framework does not mean. I'm not talking about trying to calm your child down when they're upset, or angry, or anything else—that's usually a losing battle that leaves everyone more frustrated. Children's big emotions are normal and necessary.

The mindset shift here is huge: we're not trying to settle our child down; we're giving our child tools to settle themselves. Big difference. The first approach makes you responsible for managing their emotions (exhausting, and also unsustainable), while the second empowers them with skills they can use for a lifetime. Instead of focusing on how to control your child's behavior, this approach equips them with tools to navigate their own internal landscape.

2. Connect

Once you've established (or regained) your own sense of calm and created space in your family's environment, the next step is connection. This is where joyful connection comes to life—and where you'll use the activities throughout this book to transform everyday moments with your child.

Many well-meaning approaches go off the rails here. Too often, we try to connect with children by pulling them into our adult world of words instead of meeting them where they naturally love to be: in a world of play, movement, and imagination. Think about it: how many times have you tried to explain to a four-year-old why they need to calm down, using all your grown-up words? How did that work out for you?

If your experience has been similar to mine, not great. That's because young children don't primarily process the world through verbal reasoning. They learn and experience life through their bodies, through exploring, through rhythm and imagination.

True connection with young children happens when we enter their world instead of demanding they enter ours. This is why the connection activities in this book aren't about sitting still with eyes closed (although there's nothing wrong with that, of course). They're joyful: they're about movement, music, and play. Let's unpack each.

Movement: How Children Make Sense of the World

Movement isn't just how children burn off energy—it's how they learn, process emotions, and make sense of what's happening around them. A child who seems like they're constantly in motion—jumping, spinning, wiggling—isn't being "difficult." They're doing exactly what their developing brain needs them to do.

A young child's brain develops from the bottom up—starting with basic movement and balance before they can handle complex tasks like sitting still, paying attention, or managing emotions. When kids move, their brains literally build the connections they need to handle big feelings and learn new things. Movement also helps kids figure out what their body feels like—and when they know how angry or anxious feels, they can catch those feelings before they explode.

This is why trying to get young children to sit perfectly still often backfires. When a child hasn't had enough movement, their brain works so hard just to keep their body still that there's no mental energy left to listen or follow your directions. But when we incorporate movement into mindful activities—making a giant hot-air balloon with our arms while breathing, or having a quick wiggle-dance party before settling at the table—we're speaking their language.

Movement is an incredibly powerful regulator for kids. When in doubt, get them moving! Whether your child is cranky, low energy, or not paying attention, movement can work wonders—which is why it's the basis of many activities throughout this book, including the partner activities you can do together with your child. Moving together levels the playing field, so to speak: you're both in your bodies, being a little silly, experiencing the joy of physical expression—no power dynamic at play, just shared experience in the moment.

Music: The Universal Kid Language

Music, rhythm, and song are magical for kids in all kinds of ways. Here's why they work so well:

Music naturally regulates kids' bodies and brains. It grabs children's attention and helps their bodies and emotions to settle down. A steady beat gives kids' brains something to organize around, helping them feel calmer, while listening to music releases feel-good chemicals like dopamine.

Music helps kids focus and remember. Music lights up multiple parts of a child's brain at once, making it incredibly powerful for helping them focus and retain information. When you put routine instructions—like "time to get teeth brushed and jammies on"—to a simple melody or rhythm, suddenly your child remembers them, because their brain is paying attention differently. (This works for all ages: it's why you can still sing that McDonald's jingle from fifteen years ago.)

Music creates instant connection. When you sing or clap rhythms together, oxytocin is released in both of you—the same bonding hormone that flows when you hug. It's one of the fastest (and sweetest) ways to feel deeply connected to your child.

Music creates structure and predictability. Using music as part of your daily routines—like a good morning song, toothbrushing tune, or bedtime lullaby—gives kids something predictable to count on, which feels comforting to them. Musical touchstones like this throughout the day can help transitions flow a lot more easily.

Music helps process big emotions. Music gives kids a safe way to feel and release big emotions—whether they're dancing out excitement or drumming away anxiety. It's how we all naturally process feelings (I can't be the only one who played the same sad song over and over in my room after a teenage heartbreak) and it works beautifully for children too.

Music transforms your home's atmosphere. A calm, gentle song can settle everyone down, while an upbeat tune turns cleanup time into a dance party. Having the right soundtrack for your days can truly transform the feeling of your family life. When you bring music into your daily routines with kids (and no, you don't have to be a "singer" or musician), you're not just making things easier in your home, you're creating joyful traditions your child will remember.

Throughout this book, you'll find song suggestions and rhythm activities—complete with links to audios and videos—that put this musical magic to work in everyday moments with your child.

Play: The Key to Your Child's World

Play is how our child invites us into their inner life. When your four-year-old asks you to pretend you're a dinosaur or tells you the living room couch is a pirate ship, they're offering you something precious: a glimpse into how they see the world around them.

Play isn't just what children do when they're bored or need entertainment. It's their primary language for processing experiences, working through emotions, and making sense of relationships. When we join them in their imaginative world—really join them, not just hover nearby checking our phones—we're communicating in a way that feels natural and safe to them.

This is why some of the most profound parent-child connections happen during seemingly silly moments. When you get down on the floor and genuinely engage in their pretend tea party, you're telling your child: "Your world matters to me. I want to be where you are." That message gets absorbed at a level deeper than any words could reach.

Now, I'm not asking you to spend hours on the floor pretending to sip imaginary tea—I know that's not realistic with everything else on your plate. (I'll be honest, tea parties were never my jam.) But even a few minutes of genuine presence in their world makes a huge difference. Quality over quantity.

And true play, for a child, happens when we aren't trying to make it "educational" or "productive," but when we're simply following their lead—letting them be the expert who sets the rules of their imaginary domain. Resisting the urge to teach, steer the narrative, or impose your own ideas (bite your tongue if you have to), and instead becoming curious participants in their stories creates space for authentic connection to happen.

This is why the mindful connection activities in this book are rooted in imaginative play. When our children make rainstorms on their laps or breathe like peaceful pandas, we're not just teaching them powerful techniques for calm and self-regulation—we're meeting them in the place where they feel most themselves and are most ready to learn and grow.

Joyful Connection: Secrets to Success

Every connection activity in the chapters that follow can be done in sixty seconds, is designed to delight children, and is a breeze to fit into your daily routines.

This is the winning strategy:

1. Keep it short (one minute or less).
2. Keep it kid-friendly (playful and fun).
3. Keep it consistent (attach it to something you already do every day).

I did a whole TEDx Talk on these three simple secrets to success, if you want to look it up!

Let me give you a real-life example. My daughter went through a period of intense separation anxiety when starting preschool. All my well-intentioned grown-up words about how school was safe and how I would always come back in the afternoon did nothing to ease her fears.

What finally helped was a simple little ritual we called Strings. Each morning outside the school, we'd pretend to take a piece of string from our hearts and tie them together. Then we sang a little song about how no matter how far apart we were, we stayed connected by this invisible string.

You can see the three-step formula at work here: it was short (it took less than a minute), kid-friendly (it used playful imagination), and we did it consistently (every morning before I walked her inside the school). Was it literally true? Of course not. Was it developmentally perfect for a five-year-old's magical thinking? Absolutely. It gave her a concrete, imaginative way to understand an abstract concept (emotional connection despite physical separation). And because we did it every day, it became a reliable touchstone she could mentally return to when feeling anxious.

That's the power of connection that meets children where they are. When we infuse mindful connection activities with music, movement, and play, while keeping them short and making them fun, we're not just making them more appealing—we're making them way more effective. We're creating neural pathways that link positive experiences with mindful awareness, in ways that make sense to developing brains.

When these practices become as routine as brushing teeth, they transform from "something we do" into "who we are" as a family. The real benefits come not from any single moment, but from the cumulative effect of many small, consistent practices over time. These consistent, shared moments of playful connection are relationship gold.

And when you use these tools regularly during calm, everyday moments, they become tools in your child's toolbox—already practiced and familiar—ready to be pulled out and used when a crisis hits.

3. Create

Once you've established your own calm presence and are consistently connecting with your child in ways that speak to them, you get to choose what comes next. This is where you step into your power as a parent—you decide how to reclaim your mornings, transform car rides, reimagine mealtimes, or redesign bedtimes. The Create step is entirely yours to shape. You have the ability to intentionally design the family environment you've always envisioned.

Take a beat here to dream for a moment about what your ideal home life with your child looks like, feels like, and sounds like.

Imagine:

- More joy, laughter, and genuine delight woven into your everyday moments together
- Daily routines that support everyone's well-being—and that are way more fun
- Transitions that happen more smoothly, without the usual resistance
- Feeling confident and empowered in your parenting, even during the most challenging moments
- Having a toolkit of mindful strategies ready when your child needs support most
- Building a deep, lasting bond with your child that grows stronger over time
- Creating family traditions built on joyful connection
- Preserving the wonder of childhood for your child, honoring their natural curiosity and need for exploration and play
- Knowing that the foundation you're building together will sustain your relationship for years to come

This isn't wishful thinking—it's what becomes possible when you start weaving simple mindful moments into your daily life.

Here's what I mean: One night I found myself rushing through bedtime with my young son—I wanted it to be DONE. I was exhausted, and my pillow was calling me.

My four-year-old put his hand on my cheek and said, "Mommy, do the bear." Dang it! In my rush, I'd skipped our recent nightly ritual of Bear Breath (page 170), where he pretended to be a bear hibernating for the winter, taking really long, deep breaths as I tucked him into his cozy cave. I loved that he remembered, and that he valued this tiny mindful moment enough to ask for it.

I had the wonderful realization that not only were these simple practices becoming woven into the fabric of our family life, but I was now creating the relationship I wanted with my children, one tiny connection at a time.

When you're no longer constantly reacting to what's in front of you—

when you have tools to maintain your center and connect meaningfully with your child—joy has space to emerge naturally. It's not picture-perfect, but it's real. You're creating a new kind of culture in your home.

When mindful presence becomes woven into everyday moments, it creates a foundation of emotional safety. Children learn that feelings come and go, that difficult moments pass—but connection remains. This foundation doesn't just help them navigate childhood; it prepares them for life.

The Upward Spiral: Creating Your New Cycle

Many of us are stuck repeating cycles that aren't working. Maybe it's the same kind of mealtime battles that happened in your childhood home, or the rushed, chaotic mornings that leave everyone frazzled.

These patterns didn't start with you—they've been passed down through generations of well-meaning parents who were doing their best with the tools they had. But here's the thing about cycles: they can be broken, and they can be replaced with something better.

Where are you stuck in a cycle that's not working? Is it the dinner hour when everyone's cranky and hungry? Transition times that always seem to involve tears and frustration? The way big feelings get handled, or not handled, in your home?

Whatever it is, this framework offers you a new way forward—a positive cycle to replace the one that's been spinning in your family for too long.

This Changes Everything

The Calm, Connect, Create steps aren't a one-time sequence. They form a continuous upward spiral that becomes the new family rhythm:

- The **calm** you cultivate makes deeper **connection** possible.
- Authentic **connection** gives you the foundation to **create** your ideal family environment.
- The intentional environment you **create** supports greater **calm** for everyone.

This approach creates a powerful positive feedback loop that benefits the entire family system. It works like this: When you prioritize your own groundedness, you're better able to create mindful connection with your child, and you become more present and attuned to their needs. As you respond with patience and playfulness rather than reactivity, your child begins to feel more at ease and more understood, and their behavior naturally becomes less challenging—fewer meltdowns, more cooperation, easier transitions.

As a result, you experience less stress and frustration throughout your day. With your nervous system not constantly in anxiety mode, you find yourself responding more patiently and creatively rather than reactively. Your relationship with other family members improves too, as there is less tension around parenting decisions and more shared moments of joy with your child. Siblings benefit from the calmer household atmosphere as well, often displaying less rivalry and more cooperation.

This positive feedback loop replaces the all-too-common negative spiral where your stress leads to harsher dealings with your child, which increases your child's stress, further ramping up your stress. It's called co-escalation, and it's the worst, for everybody.

Each element here strengthens the others. And with practice, this positive cycle becomes more natural, requiring less conscious effort while creating more ease and joy in your daily life with your child.

You Can Start Right Now

The beauty of this framework is that you can enter the cycle anywhere, starting right this minute. Having one of those days? Start with calming yourself. Feeling disconnected from your child? Try one of the playful connection activities. Wanting to establish a new family rhythm? Create a simple routine that incorporates mindful elements.

Wherever you begin, the other elements will naturally follow, creating momentum toward the family life you actually want.

Remember, simple doesn't mean easy, especially at first. These practices take repetition to become second nature. But there's no need for a massive lifestyle overhaul here—these three steps can be implemented in tiny moments throughout your day, starting now.

You have the power to be the one who breaks the pattern you're in and to create something different for your child. To establish new patterns that serve your family's well-being instead of depleting it.

Will there still be chaos? Absolutely. You're not raising droids. There will be tantrums and tough days and moments when everyone's mindful presence flies out the window (including yours).

But with these three simple steps consistently applied, those challenging moments become outliers rather than the defining feature of your family life.

Remember the assembly story from Chapter 1? It's these three steps—Calm, Connect, Create—in real life: I walked into that gym in a calm frame of mind (truly happy to be there, settled and grounded in my own emotional state), I connected with the children on their level (through rhythm, active movement, and play), and then I created the atmosphere I wanted (joyful, energetic, and fun—and yes, a bit loud, but under control).

I have to tell you, when I'm able to grab the complete, focused attention of hundreds of kindergartners in less than a minute, I feel like I have a superpower. Spoiler: I don't. I'm just using these three simple steps that work every time. And now you have everything you need to do it too.

It's a simple, incredibly powerful approach that works with young children's beautiful natural tendencies rather than against them.

Calm, Connect, Create in Action

Here's an example:

The Challenge: You're staring into the fridge after a long day, hoping dinner will magically present itself. Your child is squirrelly and complaining already; the situation is going downhill fast. You're anticipating the frustration you'll feel when you're trying to get them to eat what you put in front of them, or even just to stay at the table for more than forty-five seconds.

Start Your New Cycle: Rather than matching your child's negative energy and upsetness (super-unproductive), you start to create your new cycle.

Calm: You take sixty seconds to settle yourself. You have this book on your counter and remember that Kira (hi) has this What's in the Cupboard exercise (page 142, in Time to Eat) to help moms like you ground themselves and reset in this exact type of moment. You try it; one minute later, you feel way better already.

Connect: From that same Time to Eat chapter, you use a quick connection game when you sit at the table with your child: Slow Like a Sloth (page 145). They love it, the energy shifts immediately.

Create: Instead of your usual broken-record "You're not excused; please stay at the table," in between negotiating about bites, you've brought play into the moment. You've created the atmosphere at mealtime that you've been wanting, using joyful connection. Everyone feels better. It's a lot more fun.

Bonus: This book has many quick ways to center yourself, with tons of activities like the Sloth one above. So you and your child never get bored—you have plenty of ideas to try at all times of the day.

Over Time: The super-simple process above changes the game in your home. You're creating a new narrative. You're essentially the DJ of the vibe in your house, and you can play whatever you want.

Your home becomes a place where laughter happens more often, and where connection wins over correction. You don't get a pit in your stomach thinking about the bedtime routine or family dinner. You're steering this ship.

What's Next

In the chapters ahead, we'll explore practical ways to bring joyful, mindful connection into every part of your day with your child. Each chapter focuses on a specific daily rhythm—morning routines, travel time, play, meals, bedtime—with simple activities you and your child can try immediately.

The chapters are designed around the Calm, Connect, Create cycle. We'll start with simple ways to ground yourself and calm your environment, then move into activities that deepen your connection with your child, and finally look at how to use that foundation to create the peaceful, joyful moments you're dreaming of. This isn't a rigid formula; it's a gentle rhythm that builds on itself, making each step easier and more natural than the last.

Remember, you don't need to implement everything at once. Start with a practice that speaks to you and your child, try it consistently for a week or so, and notice what happens. Small shifts, applied consistently, create significant change over time.

Right now, take a moment to pat yourself on the back for being here, for caring enough about your child's well-being to explore new approaches. Go, you! That care itself is a powerful form of presence.

Here comes the practical stuff. Let's go.

Rise and Shine

Starting Your Day with Presence and Joy

BEFORE I HAD CHILDREN, I thought mornings with little ones would be full of snuggles and fun family bonding over a wholesome breakfast. I also thought I'd make all my own baby food. Hahahaha!

When my kids were seven, four, and teeny-tiny, my mornings were like this: repeating myself a million times, handling multiple mini-crises, and walking around looking for things while carrying a baby in need of a diaper change.

I remember one morning when my daughter wouldn't get dressed because her favorite super-soft velour pants were in the wash, and she wouldn't wear any others as they felt scratchy (natural next step for me: beating myself up in my head about forgetting to start the laundry the night before).

She stood in the kitchen doorway in her undies and cried her head off. It was so loud that my son couldn't hear me repeatedly ask him to sit at the counter to eat, which naturally also set the baby off screaming—and once the baby got going, all bets were off. I looked at the clock and realized that, once again, the odds of getting her to school on time were dwindling by the moment.

A few years later, my youngest's preschool teacher took me aside at a parents' night and told me mine was the only child in the class who couldn't tie his shoes on his own. I was mortified. With two older kids, I had been feeling a bit cocky, like a this-is-not-my-first-rodeo veteran, and I was beyond embarrassed to hear this.

The teacher went on to say that shoe tying is an important learning milestone and that, no matter how long it took, I needed to let him tie his shoes for himself. I was like, who has the time for that?! Our mornings were so nutty that one of his older siblings or I would tie them every single time so we could get out the door somewhere near the time we were supposed to.

Or maybe you can relate to my friend Noriko. She didn't sign her son up for the morning session of preschool, even though it would have worked better for her work schedule and her entire family's routine. Want to know why? You guessed it. Her mornings were so unpredictable that she felt she'd never get her son there on time and that she was setting herself up to fail. She let the morning chaos dictate her schedule—and believe me, I understood. Maybe you do too.

What I'm trying to say is, if your mornings feel a bit less than calm, and quite far from joyful, you're not alone. Mornings set the tone for the entire day, and when that first hour or two with your child is a s***show, your whole day can really suck.

Does it have to be this way? Nope. We deserve calm(ish), pleasant (dare I say fun?) mornings with our children. And it's possible.

What If . . .

Let's imagine for a moment that you're able to take one minute to yourself (yes, I really mean one minute) to breathe and stretch and check in with your body. You've planned, or at least thought about, breakfast the night before and laid out clothes, so those decisions are already made. Your toddler has been loving giving his Weather Report (page 46) as soon as he wakes up, and you've noticed that it has really helped improve his mood and focus his attention.

And yes, maybe the baby is crying more than usual. But since implementing simple, quick connection practices into your morning, you've found more of an ability to remain present and calm. You can handle it with relative grace and not let it stress you out or wreck the morning that you've intentionally planned. You're in charge here. Not the chaos.

That's the vision I want to help you bring to life. Let's start with some practical tips to get you there.

Setting the Stage: Tips for a Calmer Morning

It starts the night before. How can we set ourselves up for success twelve hours ahead of the morning rush? It's true that we don't know exactly what awaits us: Will the baby sleep through the night? Is the virus that's been going around going to catch up with my toddler? Will it rain and mess up our trip to the park?

Here's a strategy that can help you win the morning despite those uncertainties—eliminate as many decisions as you can the night before.

Making even small choices adds up quickly and can cause "decision fatigue," leaving us mentally exhausted, irritable, and overwhelmed by little things. (And then we're way more likely to just say yes to the kids splitting a Snickers for breakfast. Those peanuts must provide some protein, right?)

We definitely don't need to deplete our mental energy first thing in the morning. When we aren't spending our time deciding this, that, and the other thing, we're able to be much more present with our child.

Here are some simple strategies that can create remarkable shifts—I think you'll be pleasantly surprised at the lightness and ease that result when you put one or more of these into practice:

- Lay out clothes for yourself and your children, or have them do it, before bed. Get rid of the morning rush of scrambling to find outfits that are clean-adjacent and relatively unrumpled.

- Plan breakfast. Decide what you're having in advance, or maybe two easy options if you want to give your child a choice. Setting out breakfast stuff on the counter or even prepping the night before saves time and makes things feel way more relaxed in the morning.

- At bedtime, have your child pick the mindful activity you'll do in the morning, so you know you'll have that moment of real connection. There are lots to choose from (starting on page 43).
- Tidy up and minimize clutter in the rooms or spaces you'll all need to pass through in the morning. I know this one is hard at the end of the day, but it goes a long way toward creating a peaceful environment. A clean-ish and organized space really contributes to a calmer morning atmosphere.

Do what you need for yourself. Our state of calmness (or not) has a massive effect on our kids. Take a moment to really think about this one. What do you need to feel grounded and centered in the morning? Going back to the night before, can you get the coffee machine ready to go, or set up your tea? Consider what would make you feel confident and empowered as you start your day. Making a smoothie and having it waiting in the fridge? Getting your work bag packed and ready?

We've all heard the advice about getting up an hour earlier than the kids, to have plenty of time in a quiet house for self-care and all that. (I hear you: thanks for the laugh. I need SLEEP!) But tending to your own needs can also simply look like one minute to breathe in a quiet space before diving into the world of your child. (It helps. Do it in the bathroom with the door closed if you have to.)

Remember, the best gift you can give your child at the start of the day is the most calm, centered, grounded version of yourself.

Accept that you can't control everything. Part of a mindful approach to the morning (to anything, really) is accepting that certain things are just plain out of your control.

Here's how I look at it: the toaster can break AND you can lose your mind about it (and still have to deal with it), or the toaster can break and you can just deal with it. I don't mean to be dismissive about circumstances that are really challenging, but the sooner we accept that stuff just happens (pretty much constantly) that's out of our control, the better. When we let surprises or breakdowns really get to us, we're just adding stress to the situation and actually hampering our own ability to deal with it effectively.

And here's another thing: your child will remember your meltdown about the toaster far more than they'll remember the sensible talk you give them later about how even though Mommy was frustrated, she shouldn't yell or say those bad words. Kids learn from what we do far more than from what we say.

Pick your battles. In other words, what can you let go of? Sometimes we get so committed to our schedule that we end up prioritizing it over everyone's well-being—for instance, we might forget that, for the most part, the occasional missed day of school, especially in early childhood, is generally OK. It's certainly not worth pushing it if no one has slept, someone's not feeling well, or you're not going to get there until it's halfway over. It doesn't make you a bad parent; it makes you one who's made the wise decision that letting school go today is best for everyone's emotional and physical health.

Mama Mantra

Presence over pressure.

Also, does it really matter if your child goes out the door, say, in a plaid shirt and striped pants? I'll tell you, things became a lot easier for me once I let the clothes thing go. It was a little heartbreaking, for sure, when my daughter refused to let me choose (or even weigh in on) her outfits anymore and wore essentially the same four things for about a year. Still, I got over it real quick when I realized how much less time I would spend negotiating with her about it.

One of my boys had a phase where he wore a full swimmy-suit (the kind with built-in floaties) and his sister's too-big pink Crocs, often topped with a catcher's helmet (one hundred percent true). Granted, we probably couldn't have let him go to school in that, but he regularly wore it grocery shopping with me—boy, was he happy about it—and I was able to laugh along with the cashier who always complimented his outfits.

I got to the point where I embraced my kids' choosing what to wear on their own, and looked at it as a sign of their independence and character. Kids have to make their own choices, even the not-great ones, in order to develop their own identity. Plus, it makes a fun story later.

Slow down and make contact. This will make everything else go better. Take your usual morning-rush-hour speed down a few notches and offer big hugs first thing, high fives when the teeth get brushed, lots of pats on the back. Look in your child's eyes when you talk to them and listen when they talk to you. (It makes a huge difference here to minimize outside distractions and noise by turning off TVs and things that go beep.)

If you don't feel like you have time, make the time. See above, and figure out what you can let go of. Especially when there are things kids have to do: find backpacks, get shoes on, put dishes in the dishwasher—if you've spent a few moments making real, intentional contact with them, and they feel heard and seen by you, they're way more likely to get those tasks done without complaint.

This can also have the magical effect of preventing you from having to repeat yourself. Imagine that. This leads us to the next point . . .

Say less. Raise your hand if you've ever found yourself rushing around, shouting "OK, we're going! Get your shoes on!" as you dash to grab something you forgot. You come back and the shoes are still not on. You say it again while sweeping the dishes into the sink so you can enjoy doing them later. You pass by your child again and the shoes are still not on . . . my hand is up.

Now, let me ask you, and I don't mean to be snarky, but are YOU really ready to walk out the door? Probably not. I used to do this all the time. I thought that if I told the kids it was time to go while I was still getting ready, they'd get ready, and then by the time I was ready . . . Surprise! This doesn't work.

Mama Mantra

Connect, then direct.

Slow down and connect with them first. Then you can say it once and mean it. Here's how it works: Look your child in the eyes—when neither of you is doing anything else at the same time—and say, "In five minutes, it will be time to put your shoes on." Then in five minutes say, "It's time to put your shoes on." Full stop.

Important note here: Make sure you're not asking a question. "Ready to get in the car?" invites a "No!" response, even if that's not what you meant. Instead, state clearly, "It's time to get in the car." It's a statement, a clear declaration of what is happening. Remember, YOU are driving the bus, as it were. Give the instruction when it's genuinely time to do the thing and when you're actually ready yourself.

Think about your communication. Simplify your instructions and avoid overcomplicating things with unnecessary steps or extra commentary, which just make your child tune out.

Calm Starts with You

I'll try not to be annoying about this, but you'll definitely hear it more than once or twice: your mental and emotional state plays a huge part in setting the tone in your home with kids. Here are some quick, simple exercises to help you start the day with calm and intention. These are just ideas, and I am NOT saying do all of them. Pick one that appeals to you and try it in the morning for a week or so, then revisit and see how you feel about it.

And remember, this isn't an instant-relief pill—it's a practice, and one that, with consistency, really pays off.

I Am Here, It Is Now

This is about becoming truly aware of where we are and what is happening in this moment. We're not trying to change anything here–much as we might like to. We're simply observing what's going on. It won't make a not-great situation suddenly rosy, but as it shifts your focus from worry/stress/planning mode to the present moment, it may well give you a bit more equanimity and calm.

HOW-TO

Use the 3-2-1 method.

Look around you and name three things you can see. It can be anything in your immediate environment, from a glass on the table to a tree outside the window.

Take a moment to really observe each thing.

Next, focus on two things you can physically feel. It could be the softness of your sweatshirt, the warmth of your mug, or the coolness of the counter.

Pause and really feel each one.

Finally, listen carefully and identify one specific sound you can hear–it could be the refrigerator humming, distant traffic noise, or even your own breathing.

Take a few long breaths in and out.

This might feel weird, but just try it. Say to yourself (out loud or in your head): "I am here, it is now."

The Ideal Average Day

It's easy to dream about the vacation home and the trips to Paris, but regular life isn't like that. Getting clear on what our ideal "everyday" day is helps us identify what truly matters to us, clarifying our core values and priorities. It can serve as a source of inspiration and encourage us to be mindful and intentional in how we spend our time and energy.

Also, remember decision fatigue? Having a clear picture of our ideal day eliminates a lot of daily decision-making. Instead of weighing every choice from scratch, now we can evaluate choices based on whether they bring us closer to or further from what we're ideally going for. It's a valuable exercise for reducing decision overwhelm and creating a more fulfilling and intentional daily life.

HOW-TO

This exercise is best done at a time when you're not rushed trying to pack lunches, find socks, and generally manage a three-ring circus.

When you have a few moments to yourself, take a few deep breaths in and out and think about your ideal average day. (Grab a notebook or your laptop to write it down and keep it handy.)

Include all the details: what time you wake up, the first thing you do, what's for breakfast, what time you head out the door, how the car ride goes, all of it.

Use your senses as a guide: How does it sound? Is there laughter or singing? What do you feel? Take your time.

Highlight the key elements that make this day ideal, such as specific activities, the types of interactions you have with your child and with others, and how you feel throughout.

Your vision includes all the normal things that have to happen and the chores that need to be done, of course, but you're imagining them going as smoothly and easily (even pleasantly! maybe they're even fun!) as possible.

You might be surprised at how helpful this is. You'll likely get insights into changes—even tiny ones—you can make in your daily routine to create more mindful presence, peace, and calm in your day.

Commit to taking one of those tiny steps within the next week. Write it down! And keep your notes close to revisit often.

Your Child's Best Self

My son's first-grade teacher told me about this when I asked her how she was able to handle her huge, incredibly challenging class. She said that even as she was dealing with kids chucking erasers across the room, she maintained an image of their "best selves" in her mind. (My son was for sure one of the eraser-chuckers.)

This is super helpful when your child is displaying challenging or disruptive behavior. Focusing on your child's strengths and positive qualities helps you not obsess about whatever they're currently doing that's problematic, enabling you to remain relatively composed and helping you approach the situation with more compassion. Children feel secure and understood when they know their parents see and believe in their best selves, and it strengthens your bond with them. I still use it during difficult moments.

HOW-TO

Take a long breath in, then let it all the way out.

Close your eyes if that feels OK, and vividly imagine your child at their best—happy, confident, and demonstrating their positive qualities.

What do they look like and sound like, and how do they act?

Focus all your attention on your visualization, reminding yourself of your child's potential and of the bigger picture.

When you've got that picture firmly in mind, only then shift your attention to your child's current behavior, with empathy and a desire to help them learn and grow.

Connection Activities

Watch me demonstrate all of these Rise and Shine activities, songs, and rhythm games, plus get the playlist, right here!

Here are some quick and fun morning connection activities to try with your child. Designed just for young ones, these are super short and simple to fit into your established routine. Remember, it doesn't take long to be effective; consistency is the key. And don't worry if you try one and it doesn't "take" right away. Try another and keep going—practice makes progress!

You'll also find suggestions for my original songs that pair with each of these activities. As we talked about in Chapter 3, music is pure magic for young children—it naturally engages their bodies and minds while supporting their emotional regulation, which is another way of saying it helps them not lose their minds before 8 AM. The rhythm provides structure that helps organize their nervous systems, creating the predictability they crave and smoothing transitions. (And I'm sure you'd agree that anything that helps get shoes on more quickly is worth its weight in gold.)

A sweet good-morning song or upbeat tune at breakfast time can instantly shift the energy, making a potentially chaotic start feel playful instead. When you incorporate music into your morning, you're not just adding fun, you're creating a powerful touchstone that helps your child feel grounded, in control of themselves, and ready for their day.

Before you start any of these activities, be sure your space is relatively clear and distractions are at a minimum (TV off and phones out of sight, pretty please), and that you're able to be present and participate with your child for a few minutes.

Good Morning, Body!

This playful body scan helps children develop the critical skill of self-awareness as they take the time to check in with themselves instead of careening through the day on autopilot. The ability to tune in to their own bodies and recognize how they're feeling starts the day with a moment of mindful presence, and it's just the right amount of silly fun too. This works great as the first thing you do when you wake your child up!

SONG PAIRING: "Thank You, Body"

SCRIPT

Let's say good morning to our bodies.
Reach all the way down and tickle your toes. Good morning, toes!
How do your toes feel this morning?
(*Encourage children to respond to each question! You can do it too if you like.*)
Now find your knees. Oh, hi, knees!
How do your knees feel this morning?
Put your hands on your belly and give it a little rub. Hey, belly!
Take a long breath in and let it out. How does your belly feel this morning?
Put your hands over your heart. Hello, heart!
Take a breath in and let it out. How does your heart feel this morning?
Put your hands on your head, where your smart brain is.
Good morning, brain! Take a breath in and let it out. How does your brain feel this morning?
Bring your hands down. Give your whole body a little shake.
How does your whole body feel this morning?
Good morning, body!

IN THE CLASSROOM: Read the script as written without the questions, or ask students to answer the questions silently in their mind. At the end, ask students how their bodies are feeling and have them share, or invite them to write or draw their responses.

Sun Breath

Imagining they're the bright, warm sun gives children a concrete way to understand how their breath can radiate positive energy–both within themselves and outward to others. The combination of deep breathing with expressive arm movements helps shake off the morning sleepies and creates a sense of focused energy. Perfect for an empowering start to the day.

SONG PAIRING: "Shine Like the Sun"

SCRIPT

Imagine you're the sun. Take a long breath in, and as you let it out, send out your rays of sunshine.

(*Encourage and model motions here, sending out the rays of sunshine with your body.*)

Do it again. Take a big breath in, and as you let it out, send out your rays of sunshine.

Send them out in front of you and out behind you!

Send them out to the left and send them out to the right.

Send sunshine out in a HUGE circle all around you!

You're spreading sunshine everywhere!

Feel it getting brighter and warmer all around you every time you breathe in and out.

Let's have a sunny day!

IN THE CLASSROOM: Students can stand next to their desks or in a circle. Read the script and follow the exercise as written. An additional craft could be to draw or decorate paper plate "suns" to use during this activity. If you have the space and time for movement, add a sun salutation, following along with the words to my song "Dance for the Sun"!

Rhythm & Rhyme Time

Here's a rhyme that can go with Sun Breath, with or without motions. Speak it with a steady beat, set it to your own melody, or watch the video (use the QR code on page 43):

Morning Song

Good morning to the earth (*Fold forward and touch the ground.*)
Good morning to the sun! (*Reach arms up high and wave to the sun!*)
Good morning to my body (*Give a full-body wiggle.*)
Good morning to everyone! (*Open arms out wide to the world, take a long breath in, and let it out.*)

Weather Report

This fun check-in exercise helps children recognize and name what's happening inside them using a concept they naturally understand: the weather. It normalizes all emotions—from sunny days to thunderstorms and everything in between—while gently introducing the concept that feelings, like the weather, are always changing.

SONG PAIRING: "The Weather Inside"

SCRIPT

Let's take a look outside. What kind of weather are we having today? Tell me what you see!
(*Take a moment to observe the current weather with your child.*)
Now let's take a deep breath in, and let it all the way out.
What's the weather like inside you?
Do you feel sunny, or chilly, or rainy inside?
Do you feel stormy or frosty?

Or maybe you feel some other way?
(*Let your child respond about what kind of "weather" they feel inside. After they're done, you could share your own "weather" if you like.*)
Maybe you feel like a few of these all at the same time!
Any kind of weather is OK.
The weather is always changing.
It will probably feel like something different tomorrow!
Let's take another long breath in, and let it all the way out.

IN THE CLASSROOM: Have students take turns describing the weather outside. For the "weather" inside, have each student draw a picture of what they're feeling like that day. It's a really helpful way for you as an educator to get a bead on how your students are doing first thing in the morning. It would be ideal for each student to have a special notebook, sketchbook, or journal for mindfulness activities.

Today, I'm Going to Be . . .

This simple intention-setting exercise empowers children to shape their day rather than just react to it. It fits right into your morning routine, taking no extra time—do it during breakfast, while getting dressed, or in the car. When you share your own word too, it creates a lovely moment of connection. Bonus: circle back at bedtime to reflect on how your words played out, creating a sweet end-of-day ritual.

 **SONG PAIRING:** "What's the Word?"

SCRIPT
Let's take a long breath in, and let it all the way out.
Finish this sentence in your mind: "Today, I'm going to be . . ."
You could pick a word like "friendly," or "kind," or "helpful," or any other good word you like.
Pick your own good word to finish this sentence: "Today, I'm going to be . . ."

Do you want to share your word?
(*Invite your child to share. You pick a word too, and share yours!*)
Let's do our best to remember our word all day.
Let's take another long breath in, and let it all the way out!

IN THE CLASSROOM: Read the script, asking students to choose their word silently in their mind (you can invite some or all of them to share their word aloud afterward). Students can also write their word on a sticker and put it on their desk or folder, or wear it on their shirt all day. Add a check-in before dismissal to discuss how the day went with their special word.

Wake-Up Wiggle!

The antidote to morning sluggishness, this playful exercise helps children gently transition from sleepy to energized. The slow-fast-slow movement is regulating for children's bodies, and it's ideal for those mornings when your child is moving at glacial speed or when a transition has them stuck in low gear.

SONG PAIRING: "Wake Up!"

SCRIPT
Are you feeling sleepy? I am too. Let's yawn a BIG yawn.
(*Huge, exaggerated, dramatic yawn here!*)
Now even though we feel tired . . . let's wiggle one toe. Just one!
Now wiggle another toe. Keep those toes wiggling . . .
Now wiggle one finger. Hey, just one!
Wiggle another finger.
Now wiggle your arms, AND your legs, AND your middle!
Wiggle your whole body!
Keep going. WIGGLE WIGGLE WIGGLE!
Wiggle faster!
Even faster!

Now start to slow it down.
Slow it down some more.
Hold still.
Let's take a long, slow breath in, and let it all the way out.

IN THE CLASSROOM: Read the script as written and follow the exercise. Encourage lots of big movement, then take your time slowing it down, finishing with several long, slow, deep breaths to bring the group to a calm and focused state.

Rhythm & Rhyme Time

Movement paired with rhythm is incredibly effective at helping kids regulate their bodies. This one is great for listening and focus! Watch the video to see how I do it (use the QR code on page 43).

Wiggle and Stop!

Clap, clap, clap, clap, STOP!
Breathe in, breathe out.
Tap, tap, tap, tap, STOP! (*Tap two hands on your lap.*)
Breathe in, breathe out.
Stomp, stomp, stomp, stomp, STOP!
Breathe in, breathe out.
Wiggle, wiggle, wiggle, wiggle, STOP!
Breathe in, breathe out.

Together Time: Partner Connection Activity

A Really Good Day

This is like creating a mini vision board for your day. Taking a moment together to imagine and share what will make the day ahead special helps both you and your child approach it with anticipation and gratitude. It sets a joyful, connected tone that can last all the way to bedtime.

SONG PAIRING: "Brand New Day"

HOW-TO

Sit with your child—you can be side by side, facing each other, or have your child in your lap. Whatever works. Make it easy.

Take a long breath in and out together. Let your bodies be relaxed and relatively still.

Guide your child through imagining their day ahead: "Picture today in your mind. I wonder what good things might happen?"

Prompt them with realistic questions: What sounds good for breakfast today? (Give options you're OK with.) What would be fun to play? Who might you see or talk to? What's one thing you're excited about?

Encourage them to imagine the actual day ahead, focusing on the small moments and choices that could make it special.

After they've had time to share, it's your turn. Go through a set of similar questions—ones that are relevant to your day—and share what you're looking forward to.

Finish with one more long breath in and out together, plus a hug or high five.

Rise and Shine Playlist

"Thank You, Body"

A sweet parts-of-the-body song that promotes gratitude for our amazing physical selves.

"Shine Like the Sun"

High-energy and happy, with a singalong chorus that's like musical sunshine at the start of the day.

"The Weather Inside"

A gentle how-do-I-feel song that guides children to look at the weather outside and then explore the emotional "weather" within themselves.

"What's the Word?"

Choose your word of the day! A fun musical way to set an intention with your child.

"Wake Up!"

Get the energy MOVING in the morning or anytime with this upbeat, hand-clapping tune.

"Brand New Day"

A good-morning anthem that celebrates fresh starts and endless possibilities.

Your Turn

Transform Your Mornings from Chaos to Connection

You've probably imagined what it would feel like to have mornings that actually feel good—where you wake up looking forward to time with your child instead of dreading the chaos ahead. Where you're the calm, grounded parent you want to be, even when the baby's bawling and no one can find their clothes. Now it's your opportunity to intentionally create exactly that.

When you make the simple tools in this chapter part of your morning routine, you're not just doing sweet breathing exercises with your toddler. You're taking charge of the tone of your entire day.

A minute of Sun Breath here, a quick Weather Report there, and suddenly you're not at the mercy of whatever the morning throws at you. You're actively creating the calm, connected start to the day you've been wanting. Mornings might be the only one-on-one time you get with your child until bedtime; this is your chance to send them into the world feeling loved and strongly connected to a grown-up who's got their you-know-what together.

You have the power to create this—it doesn't need to depend on the weather, your child's mood, or if everything goes according to plan. With these simple tools and your intention to fully show up, you can transform your mornings from survival mode into something nourishing and meaningful for both you and your child.

When you use these Calm & Connect steps, you'll Create:

More of This

- Doing what you need for yourself
- The ease of having planned ahead
- Tiny bits of gratitude
- Letting go of battles that aren't worth fighting
- Hugs and high fives with your child
- Positivity, maybe even humor

Less of That

- Pessimism and negativity
- Rushing
- Repeating yourself
- Negotiating
- Relying on devices or screens for your child
- Resigning yourself to chaos

On the Road

From Backseat Battles to Joyful Adventures

MAYBE THIS SCENE will sound familiar: I'm attempting to muscle my three-year-old into her car seat (having walked everywhere in NYC since she was born, this is a new experience for both of us). She protests loudly and refuses, arching her back so I can't buckle her in. I try to reason with her, to explain we have to get going, it's for her safety, and all the things grown-ups think are important to say. But it's too late—the storm hits. She explodes, yelling and screaming.

I sit down in the driveway and bawl. I'm actually not sure who cries harder, my daughter or me.

My friend Suzie calls it the "battle royale," aka the Great Car Seat Wrestling Match. Not exactly a delightful way to start a road trip. And it hasn't even begun!

Traveling with young children is no joke. Raise your hand if you've ever felt like you need a vacation from your vacation? Yup, me too. It's often a serious test of patience, and the exact opposite of relaxing. I know people who just don't travel at all with their young kids, saying they're going to "wait until it's easier." I get it.

Why It's Hard

There's overstimulation, for one thing. Constant visual input, unfamiliar and abrasive noises like announcements and loud talkers. If you're on a plane or train, or in an unfamiliar car, new and strange vibrations from big engines can feel intense and unsettling. Physical discomfort comes into play too—when children can't stretch, wiggle, or get comfy, they may soon feel restless or turn into a crankypants.

Routines often go out the window while traveling, which can feel really destabilizing. Mealtimes and naps shift, sleep schedules fall apart, and you pay the price later. And although sometimes what's needed is to have children (and grown-ups) on their screens with headphones on, it can make travel feel isolating. Everyone's in their own silo doing their thing, and you're left wondering how this qualifies as a "family" trip.

Here's another biggie: rushing, which tends to accompany the intense pressure to stay on schedule or make a flight. Kids are super sensitive to the emotional temperature around them—I promise you they feel that stress.

(Has any parent ever said: "Wow, I am so ahead of the game! Everything's in the car already, I'm just going to put my feet up and take long, deep breaths with my extra ten minutes before we head out"?)

Picture the typical chaotic dash of scrambling to get bags packed, shoes on, and kids out the door, all while checking the traffic on your phone every few seconds. In situations like these, stress hormones like cortisol spike in us. Kids sense it, and they'll likely react in ways that you're not going to appreciate.

When we grown-ups feel the urge to speed things up, kids often respond the opposite way, by slowing down and digging in their heels. This push-and-pull doesn't just stall your progress forward—it sends you in a completely different direction: straight toward Meltdown City.

What If . . .

What if travel with young children could be more about joyful connection instead? Ask yourself this question: How can this road trip/bus ride/flight become an opportunity for joy and connection with my child? I'm serious—really think about it. When you shift your perspective this way, the answers that come up might surprise you.

Imagine trips to visit grandparents and even drives to school as an opportunity to reconnect rather than rush. Picture children who are excited, seeing the journey as an adventure, because you've framed it that way. You've planned ahead and communicated expectations clearly, and even if everyone isn't thrilled about the early wake-up or missed school day, you're all moving in the same direction together.

There's a feeling of camaraderie, of being part of a team, as you get ready to go. With most of the "what-ifs" accounted for, you feel good about the prep you've done, and now it's time to take things as they come, with a reasonably positive mindset for whatever lies ahead. And although this may sound cheesy, it's so true: you never know what moments will turn into the memories you'll remember the most.

When my son played travel soccer, we spent countless hours on the highway to and from practices and games. While I could have done without the endless stop-and-go traffic, I loved that time with him. Those drives became spaces for uninterrupted, meandering conversations and sharing favorite songs as we took turns choosing the music. I don't remember most of the games (sorry, honey), but those car rides were special.

Sometimes the moments we carefully orchestrate take a backseat, pun intended, to the spontaneous connections that "happen to happen" along the way—when we make space for them.

I heard a story from a dad who took his children on an epic trip to China; they saw the Great Wall and lots of other wonderful cultural and historic sites. When asked what his favorite part was, his young son said it was when they were in a taxi together and they looked out the window and saw a truck next to them with a pig in the back. THAT was his favorite memory from the trip. To CHINA.

So, you never know.

Setting the Stage: Tips for Calmer Trips

Here are some key tips to make travel time smoother and more joyful.

Lay out the plan clearly ahead of time, for everyone. Not too long ago we took a daylong trip to Philly, about an hour and a half away. The night before, I had it all planned—I'd mapped the directions and packed the snack bag—and when I reminded my son what time he needed to be in the car, he cried, "Whatttt??"

It was only then that I realized: although I had mentioned the idea a week or so before, I never told him what we were actually doing.

Bottom line here: make sure everyone is clear on the plan. Kids thrive on routine and knowing what to expect, and the unknown can bring on anxiety and overwhelm. Especially if you have a child who likes or needs to know what's going to happen, go over the plan clearly well ahead of time, and (patiently) repeat as often as needed.

My youngest likes to do this for any kind of schedule change or anything that's out of the ordinary routine. "Let's go over the plan," he'll say. It makes him feel better about what's ahead. (Make sure you're clear with your partner and any other involved grown-ups too.)

When kids understand the sequence of events—such as when they need to wake up, what they'll eat, or how long the subway ride will be—it provides a sense of control and predictability, giving them a feeling of safety in a situation that might otherwise feel out of their hands.

As you go over the plan, acknowledge your child's feelings about it and let them know that it's OK to have mixed emotions. They may not be as excited as you are, or the opposite, and that's OK. This can be hard if you're really fired up about the trip and they're not—but do your best not to let your own feelings get in the way of hearing theirs.

Connect with your child on what's coming up for them—yes, plane rides can be bumpy; yes, long lines can be boring—in a matter-of-fact way, without indulging complaining. Then you can add your "and . . .": And, the pilots will get us there safely. And, we can play games during the wait in line. You get the idea.

Ask what part of the trip they're most excited about, or nervous about, or if they have any questions. (Do this when you have plenty of time to hear their answers.) You're showing that you're truly paying attention and that you're interested in what they think—a huge part of a strong bond.

Backing up a step: when you're building out the schedule, add as much buffer time in the transitions as you can. Think you'll need an hour to get out of the house in the morning? Plan on an hour and a half at least. Give yourself enough time to avoid that sense of rushed chaos (see above on how rushing stresses everybody out). Nail those transitions. You will feel so good about this.

Also, and this is huge: you're teaching your child that time and energy can be managed thoughtfully, that our state of mind doesn't have to become a victim to the traffic or the other external stuff we can't control. This tells your child, "We have time to enjoy this," and reinforces that calm and connection come first.

Create anticipation and make it feel special. Put some effort into getting fired up for the trip. You could create a trip countdown with a calendar and let your child mark off the days as it gets closer, or use a visual schedule with pictures. If you're traveling far, use a globe or book, or look online at pictures of where you're going. Make a fun and colorful packing list. I still make packing lists for my kids, and they're way past needing them. We all just like it; it gets us fired up for the adventure ahead.

Remind your child of the fun things that are coming—that you'll be seeing their funny uncle or that your airport gate has that play area (please bring hand sanitizer). Get them excited about the little things that you know will sound fun to their ears—like, "We're not going to eat breakfast at home tomorrow morning, we'll find something yummy at the bakery near Grandpa's!"

My kids were always highly motivated to get to the airport because they knew they could each pick their own pack of gum at the gift shop if we got there with enough time to spare. I know, super exciting, right?

Bring a "We're in this together!" vibe. Coming home from a trip to the Midwest one summer, we missed our connecting flight. My husband, daughter, and younger son got the last three seats on the next plane home, but my

A note on daily commutes

You can create anticipation for your daily back-and-forth to school or childcare too. What about theme days? Music Mondays, where your child picks the songs (or you make up one together), Teddy Bear Tuesdays, where your child's favorite stuffed animal joins you on the ride, or Wacky Wednesdays, where you only talk in silly voices.

Create special, shared rituals for these trips, like having a Question of the Day ("If you could be any animal, what would you be?") or a phrase you always say ("Remember how awesome you are!") toward the trip's end. On the way home each day, you could play a game like Rose, Thorn, and Bud (your "rose" is something that was awesome, your "thorn" is something that didn't go well, and your "bud" is something you're looking forward to).

On our long drive to school each morning, my son and I used to play the Flag Game, which was simply counting the flags we'd see on people's porches (where we live, people put flags out for all the things–the seasons, holidays, Groundhog Day, you name it). It was fun and made the ride go quickly, and it was always exciting when we spotted a new flag.

older son and I were stuck late at night in the Detroit airport. It became an epic adventure. We got chips and granola bars for dinner just as the vendors were putting their gates down, and after an endless wait to talk to an agent, we finally got put up in the airport Westin to sleep for a few hours. We woke up early, had a fancy hotel breakfast, and ran to catch our flight home. The whole thing had a feeling of the two of us against the world (or at least the airline industry). He and I still talk about it.

Frame the trip as a shared adventure. As you preview the trip with your child, you're not just talking about logistics; you're creating a "We're on the same team" feeling. Making kids feel like part of the process gives them a sense of ownership (not to mention, it helps encourage them to cooperate on things like packing backpacks and getting up early).

Get their input and ideas now—when they're NOT tired, hangry, or in meltdown mode—about how "we're" going to deal with setbacks like, say, a long wait on a stopped train. They'll be way less frustrated and feel more resilient when it happens.

Mama Mantra

We're on the same team.

And give kids some agency in the process. Where can they be in charge? Even if it's as small a thing as what kind of sandwich to pack for the ride, kids thrive when they feel like they have an important role to play.

Creating this sense of unity ahead of time dramatically increases everyone's ability to adapt to less-than-ideal circumstances and makes it way more likely that you'll all be able to laugh about bumps in the road (literally and figuratively) rather than lose it. These are the moments that strengthen your family's emotional connection.

Have a "Mommy Meltdown." Let me explain! Basically, you're acting out your (exaggerated) Big Feelings as an effective way to head off a real meltdown.

Here's how this goes: You're heading toward the security line at the airport and see that it's insanely long. It looks like you'll be standing in it until the end of time, and you feel your frustration building. Knowing that children pick up on emotional tension, and anticipating a less-than-happy reaction to the wait, you get ahead of it by having a highly melodramatic (pretend) "meltdown" of your own.

Say something like, "Ooooh my gosh, what am I going to do in this long line? No no no no no! It's too long! It's so boring! It will take foreverrrr!! I can't do it, no no no!!" (Embellish and add dramatic body language as you see fit.)

This does two things. First, the surprise of it totally distracts kids from their own frustration or complaints. By intentionally having a playful meltdown yourself, you change up the usual script and break the tension in a lighthearted way. Now you've shifted the focus to a shared, funny moment—and humor is an incredibly powerful tool for defusing stress.

Second, it completely flips the usual power dynamic. Instead of being the parent in charge, you're giving your child a chance to be the one who helps and soothes. What a fun confidence booster! It gives them a sense of control, which is particularly empowering in situations where they might be feeling anxious or frustrated themselves. Children love feeling like they have a role to play. You're giving them a chance to "rescue" you!

When I used to do this, my daughter would immediately forget about her tired feet and her boredom and would go right into caregiver mode: "It's OK, Mommy! I'll get you a snack out of my backpack and we'll play a fun game in the line, OK? Do you need a hug?"

Here's a bonus benefit of this slightly subversive technique: it helps kids practice emotional intelligence. They learn how to comfort, how to practice empathy, and how to problem-solve, all of which build their social-emotional skills.

The "Mommy Meltdown" works particularly well, and I say this with love, for bossypants-type children (like my oldest).

Get clear on screen time. Well before the trip, decide with your partner or other grown-ups who are along how and when screens will come into play. Some families avoid screens altogether, some find saving screen time for the last stretch of the journey works wonders, and for some, traveling means all bets are off and kids can have at it.

Talk through expectations with your travel companions—and then with your child—so you're on the same page and no one feels caught off guard. Make it super clear ahead of time, and adjust if and when you need to. You're in charge.

When I was really little, road trips meant hanging out in the "way back" of the station wagon. Some of those trips were incredibly boring, but without screens (or, apparently, any concern around seatbelts), many, many other trips were full of made-up games and giggles that my siblings and I still remember.

Screen time often gets ramped up when traveling with kids, and I get it—devices can be a lifesaver on long trips and sometimes are exactly what's needed to keep the peace. No shame here. And this is also true: when we can swap the screen for a bit of real-life road trip magic, it's amazing how the trip starts to feel less about surviving from point A to point B and more about enjoying being together. We stay in the present moment, where opportunities for connection are right in front of us.

Calm the environment. No matter how you're traveling, a relatively clean, calm, and organized space can go a long way in reducing stress for everyone.

If you're driving, take the time before hitting the road to tidy up the car and clear out clutter. You're probably thinking, "What's the point? Do you not know how gross a backseat gets on a long road trip with young kids?" Yes, I definitely do. Still, starting off with an organized space—and doing a quick tidy at pit stops—makes a huge difference in how everyone feels. A pre-trip clean-out of your own bag can also help you feel prepared and in control.

Even in a shared space where you can't control everything, keeping the space around you clean and trash-free can be a major stress reducer, creating your own little island of calm.

Don't forget to manage comfort and temperature too. In the car, adjust the climate so everyone feels cozy. For sensitive kids, small adjustments like a cooler or warmer setting or lowering the fan can be game changers. On public transportation, think about what you can bring that will ease those sensory needs and provide comfort—your child's favorite cozy blanket, a fidget spinner, or noise-canceling headphones.

This isn't about coddling; it's about making the journey as pleasant as possible for everyone, yourself included.

Loosen up on set schedules. Clinging to home routines while traveling is a square-peg-in-a-round-hole situation—it usually leads to frustration for everyone involved. If your entire focus is on getting your toddler their 1 PM nap when you're in the back of a cab driving through a new city, you're going to miss the forest for the trees, as they say.

When we release our death grip on schedules, we often find that our children are lots more adaptable than we give them credit for. They can have a late dinner or stay up past their usual bedtime without turning into monsters. Model embracing the moment, and be Fun Mom who lets the usual rules slide this once. The world won't end if they eat dessert first or go to bed when you do. Part of a mindful, joyful travel experience with children is embracing the fact that a little spontaneity usually makes for a really fun trip.

Pack a "Happy Traveler" bag. Trips with young kids go so much more smoothly when you're well prepared with the essentials: healthy snacks, plenty of water, and fun stuff to do. Keeping little ones' bellies full wards off the hangries and prevents meltdowns before they start. Making snacks feel a little bit special—which can be as simple as cutting apples into fun shapes or using a colorful container—turns the ride into a mini celebration.

Don't underestimate the power of the (well-timed) snack as a distraction either: my friend Suzie discovered that handing her daughter a little bite just as she was being buckled into her car seat worked like fairy dust, turning that usual struggle into a much easier moment.

Water is equally important—staying hydrated keeps everyone from feeling irritable and sluggish, especially on longer trips (this is critical for you too).

Have low-tech games on hand, and maybe pack a few little unexpected items, like a new travel puzzle or card deck, doling them out when needed along the way. Come up with some fun open-ended questions that can turn a long ride into a memorable conversation. ("If you could live in any book or movie, what would it be and why?") A playlist of family favorites or an audiobook of stories children can settle in and listen to can turn even a long drive into quality time.

You can't control everything, but your Happy Traveler kit will go a long way toward making your trip more fun, joyful, and connected—while minimizing the chances of crankiness and tears.

Prepare for the "what-ifs." In my house, kids get sick on Friday at 5 PM, on the eve of a major holiday, or the moment we step onto the plane. I always pack a small emergency kit—mine is a repurposed toiletry bag with a pain reliever, an antibiotic ointment, Band-Aids, a thermometer, and Benadryl (my son will get a hamburger-sized welt on his skin if a mosquito simply flies by). Oh, and plastic bags for gross or wet things.

What would be super helpful to have if your child gets a sore throat, fever, or upset stomach? Having a small quantity of the essential emergency items you might need on hand creates serious peace of mind (and basically ensures no one will get sick).

Of course, bring extra diapers and wipes—and pro tip: make sure they stay with whoever has the baby. If you get separated by fifteen rows on the plane at the last minute and your partner has the wipes but YOU are holding the poopy toddler? I'm sorry. I've been there, and they may have had to throw away that plane.

Shift your mindset. Here's how I used to look at traveling with kids: it's basically all the same chores you have to do at home—they're just harder, because you don't know where anything is.

All true to some extent. But if you want to survive this trip and maybe even enjoy it, a more positive mindset is essential. You're setting the tone here. A mostly calm, positive attitude can transform the whole shebang and helps everyone stay more relaxed and open to whatever delightfully unpredictable adventure lies ahead.

I'm sure you've heard the saying that goes something like this: you can't choose your external circumstances, but you can always choose your response to them. Nowhere is this more true than when traveling with young kids.

Here's one way to approach it:

> The airport is a maze of long lines and confusion, and you're already running late. Your toddler is fussy, pulling at your hand, and your preschooler is asking all the questions at once. You're juggling suitcases, snacks, and beloved blankies, hustling the kids as fast as their little legs can go, and keeping an eye on the departure board. You realize there's no way you'll make it to the gate on time.
>
> You glance at the screen: the flight is delayed fifteen minutes, which in your experience is just the start of many more delays. What if you miss your connection? Will you get rebooked? The kids haven't had lunch! The little one will never nap in the airport! All you want is to get on that plane and sink into your phone with earbuds in. You feel the frustration rising, wishing you had planned better, that the kids could shush for a minute, that someone else would magically swoop in and deal with this . . .

Here's the exact same scenario—literally the only difference is your mindset around it:

Though it's been a whirlwind morning, there's a sense of adventure in the air. You're running a little behind, but you're focused on staying calm. Your toddler tugs at your hand and your preschooler is asking endless questions, and you intentionally take a deep breath. This is part of the journey—chaotic, yes, but also full of sweet moments.

You look at the time and realize you might not make it to the gate right when boarding starts. It's all part of the adventure of traveling with littles. Your kids are excited, curious, and full of energy—that's a good thing! You chat with them, pointing out fun things like a little dog in a carrier. Then you see that the flight is delayed by fifteen minutes. Perfect! Just enough time to make it to the gate without the stress of trying to get two young children to sprint full out. You focus on the things that are going right: you're together, you're safe. Maybe the little one will be just fine without a nap today. It won't be perfect, but who cares?

Mama Mantra

Mindset matters.

The kids are paying attention and learning from you, whether you think they are or not. With your language, behavior, and tone, you're modeling how to handle not only today's setbacks, but also tomorrow's potentially lost luggage, traffic, and missed bus.

I know I've said this before, but it bears repeating: children tend to do what you DO, not what you say to do!

Calm Starts with You

Creating a mindful, joyful travel experience with your child begins with you. Young kids naturally mirror the energy and emotions of the grownups around them, so a calm and present parent sets the tone for a smooth journey.

Here are some quick, simple ways to help you stay grounded in the moment when you're on the road with your child. This mindful awareness will help keep you from getting lost in stress or distraction. Choose what works for you and let go of the rest.

Body Scan

This is a mindful check-in with your physical self. By focusing on different parts of the body and consciously relaxing them, we distract the mind from worry and encourage a sense of calm. The scan can also help reduce muscle tension and increase our awareness of what's going on in our bodies—which results in us taking better care of ourselves (nudge, nudge).

A key piece here is to observe your physical body with curiosity as to how you're feeling. No judgment!

HOW-TO

Take a few long breaths in and out, and allow your breathing to settle into a steady rhythm.

Bring your attention to your feet, and notice any sensations, such as tingling, warmth in your toes, or pressure. (If you don't feel anything really, that's OK—just notice that.)

Shift your focus to your lower legs, observing any feelings of tension or relaxation. Continue up to your knees and upper legs, taking your time to notice any sensations.

Keep moving. As you go, if you notice any areas of tightness, pause for a moment. Imagine breathing into those areas to release the tension.

Bring your awareness to your hips and back, noticing any pressure points or areas of tightness, then to your stomach, noticing its rise and fall with each breath. Move up to your chest and shoulders, observing how your breath affects these areas too.

Focus on your hands, arms, and shoulders. Take your time to feel any tension or relaxation. See how your throat and neck feel, noticing any tightness or ease, then move to your jaw and facial muscles. Consciously relax these areas if you notice any tension.

By the way, it's totally normal for your mind to wander. It would be weird if it didn't. Try not to get frustrated; just gently bring your focus back to the body part you were concentrating on, without judgment.

When you're done, bring your awareness to your body as a whole and finish with a few long, deep breaths.

Tension Busters

Traveling with (or without) kids can leave us feeling physically stiff and fatigued. We hold tension in our bodies without realizing it, especially when our focus is on managing the drama in the backseat. Common places for this tension are the shoulders, neck, lower back, and hips—muscles tighten as we sit for long periods, leading to discomfort or even pain. Simple seated stretches can help by gently releasing this built-up tension, promoting better circulation, and improving flexibility, with a side benefit of reducing feelings of tiredness. Here are three to try.

Stop Sign: Extend one arm straight out in front of you, palm facing out as if you're saying "Stop." With your opposite hand, gently pull your fingers back toward your body, feeling a stretch along your forearm. Hold for a few breaths in and out, then switch hands. Rolling the wrists out can feel really good here too.

Twister: Sit tall and gently place your left hand on the outside of your right thigh. Inhale and lengthen your spine, and as you exhale, twist your torso to the right, looking toward your right shoulder. Hold for a few long breaths in and out, then gently unwind and repeat on the other side.

Ankle Alphabet: While you're sitting, lift one foot off the ground and "draw" the letters of the alphabet with your big toe, gently rotating your ankle as you go. Switch to the other foot. This helps improve circulation and is great to do when you're sitting for a long time.

S.T.O.P. Break

I'm not sure who came up with this acronym, but thank you to them for making it so easy to remember. This is a super-quick tool to practice anytime, particularly when you're feeling rushed or frustrated. It takes less than a minute but can help bring you some clarity and calm in the midst of chaos.

HOW-TO

S = Stop

Literally just pause whatever you're doing (and thinking about). This doesn't mean you have to freeze—just take a brief moment to reset your attention.

T = Take a Breath

Take a slow, deep breath in through your nose, allowing your lungs to fill. Hold for a second or two, then exhale slowly through your mouth. Feel free to repeat this a couple of times. Focusing on your breath helps bring your awareness back to your body and the present moment.

O = Observe

With your next inhale, observe how you're feeling. What's going on inside your mind and body? Are you tense? Anxious about something? Calm? Notice any thoughts or emotions without judgment. You don't need to fix anything right now—just acknowledge what's present.

P = Proceed

After taking a moment to stop, breathe, and observe, carry on with what you were doing—hopefully with more grounded energy and a bit more clarity in your mind.

Connection Activities

Watch me demonstrate all of these On the Road activities, songs, and rhythm games, plus get the playlist, right here!

Here are some short and sweet mindful activities to try with your child when you're on the road. Remember, it's about joy and connection here, so no need to force anything. If one doesn't resonate, move on and try the next. And when you find one that works, build it into your road trip routine every time, so it's part of the traveling tradition!

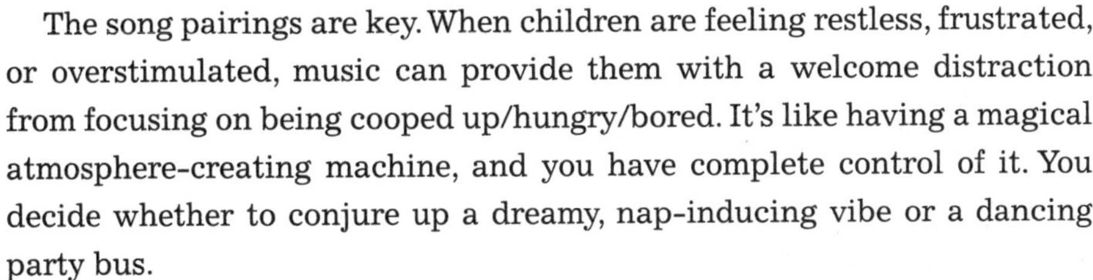

The song pairings are key. When children are feeling restless, frustrated, or overstimulated, music can provide them with a welcome distraction from focusing on being cooped up/hungry/bored. It's like having a magical atmosphere-creating machine, and you have complete control of it. You decide whether to conjure up a dreamy, nap-inducing vibe or a dancing party bus.

Since music has the unique ability to create strong emotional associations, maybe you come up with a road trip playlist or a single song that plays each time you hit the road—I guarantee it will be remembered for a long time. The difference between a whiny, tense car ride and one where the kids are car-seat-dancing in the back can be a matter of the right tune.

Outside Inside

This mindful listening exercise naturally anchors children in the present moment by focusing their attention on sounds, starting with distant noises and gradually moving inward to their immediate surroundings. It helps them develop focused attention while fostering awareness of their current environment, which creates a sense of grounding when they're feeling restless or overwhelmed.

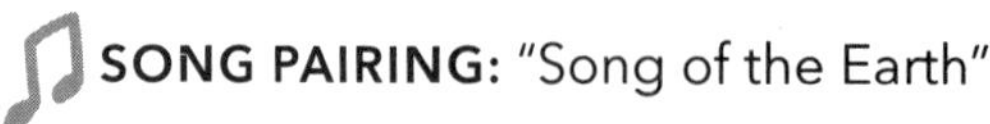

SONG PAIRING: "Song of the Earth"

SCRIPT

Let's listen to what's going on around us.
Hold your body still.
Take a long breath in, and let it out.
If you want to, you can close your eyes.
Listen to the sounds outside.
What's the farthest-away sound that you can hear?
(*Invite your child to share their answers.*)
Can you hear a plane way up high, or birds in the trees?
Do you hear music playing, an engine humming, or the wind whistling by?
Listen.
Take a long breath in, and let it out.
Now listen to the sounds inside.
What do you hear?
Is your belly making any noises?
Can you hear the sound of your breathing, or your heart beating?
Listen.
Take a long breath in, and let it out.

IN THE CLASSROOM: Guide students through listening to distant sounds (hallway noises, outdoor sounds), then classroom sounds (air conditioning, rustling papers), and finally internal sounds (breathing, heartbeat). Use as a reset during transitions or as a focus activity before tests or challenging work. Dim the lights if you can, and speak slowly, with pauses for listening.

Rhythm & Rhyme Time

Here's a rhyme that puts a new spin on the classic I Spy game. Instead of colors, you could also do shapes or anything else, like license plates from different states. (To watch the video, use the QR code on page 69.)

I Spy Song

I looked around
and you know what I found?
I found something . . . green!
Can you find it?
Tick-tock, tick-tock, tick-tock!

(*Repeat with other colors, shapes, or whatever you like!*)

Hot-Air Balloon

Help your child learn a powerful self-regulation technique without them even realizing it: the quick inhales followed by slow exhales in this exercise naturally help children relax when they're feeling wound up or anxious. The arm movements give them something physical to do (perfect for wiggly kids while still doable in a car seat), and the playful visualization makes it fun. Extend it by asking your child where their balloon is taking them, creating a magical story together around wherever they want to go.

♫ **SONG PAIRING:** "Up in the Air"

SCRIPT

Let's go on a hot-air balloon ride!
You can take your balloon anywhere you want.
(*Invite your child to share where they'd like to go.*)
Take quick, short breaths in through your nose: sniff, sniff, sniff, sniff, sniff.

As you breathe in, lift your arms out to the sides and up toward the sky.
You're filling up your balloon with air so it can fly!
Breathe out slowly, and bring your arms back down.
Do it again!
Take quick, short breaths in through your nose: sniff, sniff, sniff, sniff, sniff.
Lift your arms out and up.
Breathe out, and bring your arms back down.
Do it again, as many times as you want.

IN THE CLASSROOM: Students can sit or stand as you guide them through the script as written. The movement helps engage wiggly kids, while the breathing pattern naturally reduces stress and anxiety. Use this any time the energy feels scattered and students need to settle.

Chugga-Chugga Train

A train theme always hits: this playful breathing exercise gives restless kids a fun vocal outlet while the contrast between fast and slow keeps their attention, and the long breaths are calming. Turn it into a longer imaginative journey by repeating it as many times as your child likes, adding train whistle sounds or circular "freight train" arm motions, or asking what the train is carrying and where it's headed.

SONG PAIRING: "On the Train"

SCRIPT
Let's get our train moving down the tracks!
We'll start slowly.
Breathe in, and slowly say "Chuuuugga Chuuugga Chooooo . . ."
FAST TRAIN! Breathe in. Super fast, say "CHUGGA CHUGGA CHUGGA CHUGGA CHUGGA CHUGGA CHOO!"
Slow train.
Breathe in, and slowly say "Chuuuugga Chuuugga Chooooo . . ."
Reeeally slow train. Take a long breath in.
"C h u u u u g g a C h u u u g g a C h o o o o o . . ."

Time for our train to STOP!
Hold very still.
Breathe in, and breathe out!

IN THE CLASSROOM: Use this after recess, PE, or lunch to help students settle back into learning mode. Have students stand near their desks and follow along with the varying speeds, or organize them into "train cars" by having them place their hands on the shoulders of the person in front, creating a train that moves around the room.

Heart Breath

The ability to find a moment of calm in the middle of chaos is a valuable life skill to teach our children. This short and sweet exercise helps children create their own little pocket of peace no matter how busy their surroundings might be. The physical gesture of hands on heart activates their body's natural calming response, and the simple phrase gives them concrete words to anchor to when they're feeling stressed or overstimulated. Perfect for travel days when there are lots of transitions, new places, and sensory overload.

SONG PAIRING: "I Can Rest"

SCRIPT

Sometimes things can feel kind of stressful.
Especially when you have to go to lots of different places.
Maybe you have to be in the car, or on the bus, or on the train. That's a lot!
(*Adjust this sentence to suit your current travel situation.*)
Even when it's busy around you, you can take a little rest.
Put both hands over your heart.
Close your eyes if you want to, or look down toward your lap.
Take a long breath in, and let it all the way out.
Say "I can rest."
Take a long breath in, and let it all the way out.

Say "I can rest."
Take a long breath in, and let it all the way out.
Say "I can rest."
Take a long breath in, and let it all the way out.

IN THE CLASSROOM: Teach this as an independent coping tool students can use any time they feel stressed, or use it with the whole class when a calming moment is needed. Create a visual cue like touching your heart so students can recognize when to use this technique, and remind them that it works even when the room feels busy or chaotic. Adapt the words as you like; another good phrase to try is "I am calm."

Red Light, Green Light

This pretend "driving" game teaches your child how to regulate their energy and practice self-control through play. By switching between driving fast, driving in slow motion, and complete stops, they're learning to consciously shift between different energy levels, a key skill for managing big emotions and impulsive behaviors. The familiar concept of traffic lights makes it fun and easy to remember—you can encourage them to use this "red light/stop/breathe" technique in real situations when they need to pause and reset. Since it's done seated, it's great for real car rides, plane trips, or really anywhere.

SONG PAIRING: "Go Plane Go"

SCRIPT

Hop into your pretend car, and hold on to the steering wheel.
Green light! Go!
Drive your car fast! (*Make steering wheel motions quickly back and forth.*)
Red light! STOP. (*Freeze!*)
Breathe in, and breathe out.
Breathe in, and breathe out.
Green light! Go!
Drive your car fast! (*Make steering wheel motions quickly back and forth.*)

Red light! STOP. (*Freeze!*)
Breathe in, and breathe out.
Breathe in, and breathe out.
Yellow light! Drive slooowly. (*In exaggerated slow motion, make steering wheel motions.*)
How slowly can you drive?
Red light! STOP. (*Freeze!*)
Breathe in, and breathe out.
Breathe in, and breathe out.

IN THE CLASSROOM: This can be done seated or standing and helps teach classroom self-control. Lengthen it to give students lots of practice shifting between high energy and calm focus. Use for smoothing transitions or as a brain break between lessons.

Rhythm & Rhyme Time

This rhythm-based rhyme is perfect for car rides—the steady beat, arm motions, and fun sounds help focus the attention of restless kids while giving them a contained outlet. You can watch me do it in a video—use the QR code on page 69.

Road Trip

Road trip! (*Clap clap.*) How we gonna get there?
Road trip! (*Clap clap.*) I'll tell you how we get there!
We're gonna drive in our car—beep beep! (*Honk your horn.*)
We're gonna fly on a plane! (*Arms out wide to make wings.*)
We're gonna ride on our bikes! (*Brrring-brring.*)
We're gonna jump on a train! (*Choo, choo!*)

Together Time: Partner Connection Activity

Face Party

This silly face game is the perfect antidote to long car rides or cranky travel moments. It naturally releases tension and gets the giggles going, while all the facial movement actually helps you and your child wake up your brains and bodies when you've been sitting still. You can do this anywhere: in the backseat, at a rest stop, while waiting in line. Make sure you dive all the way in—it will instantly lighten the mood, and your child will love seeing you be just as silly as they are.

SONG PAIRING: "The Shimmy" (Rhythm-based, silly, and fun—just press play and follow along with the words!)

SCRIPT

(*Do all of this together with your child!*)

Open your eyes wide, and blink them three times.

Blink! Blink! Blink!

Wiggle your eyebrows up and down.

Wiggle your nose like a bunny!

Open your mouth really wide, and wiggle your jaw back and forth.

Stick your tongue out as far as it will go! Wiggle your tongue all around.

Can you make a fishy face?

Make any kind of silly face you want!

Wiggle your whole head around.

Now hold your body still. Take a long breath in, and let it all the way out.

Smile!

On the Road Playlist

"Song of the Earth"

A lush, dreamy celebration of the sounds of nature.

"Up in the Air"

Soaring and whimsical, for road trip daydreaming.

"On the Train"

The ultimate toe-tapping train song!

"I Can Rest"

Soothing and mantra-like, to help your child find a moment of calm anywhere.

"Go Plane Go"

Perfect for kids who love trains and planes, with a freeze-dance-inspired "Stop!" and "Go!" section.

"The Shimmy"

Catchy rhymes, easy-to-follow movement cues, and a sweet chorus of kids all set to the infectious beat of a djembe.

Reclaim the Joy in Family Travel

You've probably spent plenty of trips feeling like a referee/entertainment director/crisis manager all while trying to navigate the actual logistics of getting somewhere. Maybe you've imagined what it would be like if travel time with your child could actually be enjoyable instead of something to endure—and now you're equipped to create exactly that.

Think about it: How often do you get uninterrupted time with your child, away from home's distractions? No laundry pile staring at you, no stacks of work on your desk. This is your chance to create those moments that become treasured memories. You never know which simple moment will stick in your child's mind—and it might not be the carefully planned destination.

Using the tips and practices in this chapter, you can transform travel time from a source of stress into an opportunity for real, joyful connection. You can choose to see the journey as part of the adventure, not just the obstacle between you and your destination.

You have the power to reframe every trip, whether it's the daily drive to school or a flight across the country. You get to decide if this journey feels like a chore or an opportunity. So buckle up, Mama, and go create the road trip vibes you've always wanted.

When you use these Calm & Connect steps, you'll Create:

More of This

Anticipation for the trip

Clear expectations all around

Special, shared rituals and traditions

Wonder and appreciation

Easing up on timelines and schedules

A "We're on the same team" vibe

Less of That

Moving on autopilot

Stressing about what's out of your control

Constantly being plugged in (you or your child)

Complaining about inconveniences

Rigidity around meal and sleep schedules

Attachment to how things "should be"

Brain Boosters

Fun Ways to Help Kids Focus and Listen

NICOLE FELT LIKE she was pretty much nailing the parenting thing. Then her husband's job relocated the family across the country in February, and all of a sudden she was homeschooling her two young girls—it seemed like the easier option than throwing them into new schools midyear.

Having never been the one teaching them all day, Nicole came face-to-face with something that caught her completely off guard: just how challenging it can be to capture and hold young children's attention. She'd start explaining where Ohio was to her five-year-old, only to realize her three-year-old had abandoned the "quiet activity" Nicole had set up and was chasing the cat while belting out "Happy Birthday" at top volume. The children couldn't focus on schoolwork for more than a few minutes without getting distracted, and Nicole thought she might lose her mind.

Unfortunately, as we've all discovered when it comes to children, having a captive audience doesn't necessarily mean having an attentive one. Whether you want to have a quick family meeting about weekend plans, get your child to follow a morning routine, or simply remember their ONE chore of feeding the dog, the reality is that kids' developing brains are naturally wired to be curious and exploratory—which is incredible for learning, but can make sustained focus feel nearly impossible when you're trying to pack up and get out the door.

What Nicole was experiencing wasn't a parenting failure—it's the reality of modern childhood. Getting kids to pay attention has always been a challenge, but it's genuinely become harder in recent years. Let's look at what's behind that.

Why It's Hard

The number one challenge I hear in every workshop, parent meeting, and teacher training I lead isn't tantrums, sleep issues, or picky eating (though those are definitely up there). Over and over, parents and educators roll their eyes and tell me various versions of the same thing: "I just can't get them to pay attention!"

This isn't surprising when you consider how different childhood is today. I remember long days of wandering in the woods with my brother as a child, playing elaborate games of Family, or just being bored out of our minds—a good and healthy thing, it turns out. Those extended periods of doing one (screen-free) thing at a time are rare these days, and that's just one of the reasons that our children's ability to concentrate—there's really no other way to say it—is under assault.

A number of factors are at play here:

- **Children aren't getting enough movement.** Our brains evolved to learn while moving, yet on average children today sit for more than seven hours daily and get less than half their needed physical activity. When young children are required to sit still for longer than is appropriate for their age, their mental energy goes to "Don't wiggle, don't wiggle, don't wiggle," and that's pretty much all they can pay attention to.

  Basically, it's physiologically impossible for children to both hold their bodies relatively still for any length of time AND listen to your directions. A five-year-old is truly not meant to sit at a desk all day. Don't even get me started on this.

I say this over and over again when I talk to parents and educators: for children, movement isn't a break from learning. It IS learning.

- **Technology fragments children's attention spans.** (You saw this one coming, I'm sure.) When using a device like an iPhone, a child switches tasks every sixty-five seconds on average, training their brains to expect constant novelty. Algorithms and notification systems are specifically designed to keep kids scrolling and clicking. (If you'd like to feel terrified about this, read these books: *Stolen Focus* by Johann Hari or *The Anxious Generation* by Jonathan Haidt, which I mentioned in Chapter 1.)

- **Distracted grown-ups.** OK, I'm calling us out: we adults sometimes (often? frequently?) model unfocused behavior. When parents and caregivers constantly check phones or multitask, forgoing eye contact or responding absentmindedly while looking at a screen, children internalize that scattered attention is normal. A 2023 study in *JAMA Pediatrics* found that children were 20 percent more likely to show attention problems when parents frequently used phones during interactions with them. Yikes.

- **Inadequate sleep and downtime.** Between packed schedules, late or inconsistent bedtimes, and screens before sleep, many kids aren't getting the deep rest their developing brains need to build the capacity to focus.

  But it's not just about nighttime sleep—kids need mental rest during their waking hours too. Our children desperately need periods of doing absolutely nothing. Just being, instead of doing. True restorative downtime does not include screens, instructions, lessons, or grown-up-led activities. (Sorry!) It means giving kids mental white space: a pile of picture books, time for unstructured play, a soft blanket on the couch.

  And if they're bored, guess what? You don't need to entertain them. It's not your job—you have plenty to do. (Or, let them know the toilet needs scrubbing, and see what happens.)

With so many distractions competing for our kids' attention, getting them to tune in can seem impossible. If you feel like that clown on the tiny bike in the circus, pedaling in tiny circles, you're not alone.

This is serious business. The impact of attention struggles goes way beyond kids forgetting to put their plate in the dishwasher even though you asked them four times. The research is quite clear on this: when children can't maintain focus, they can miss crucial milestones in early learning, and these gaps widen over time.

The ripple effects can touch every part of their lives. Essential executive functions—basically, life skills like planning, organizing, and problem-solving—are negatively affected. Repeated corrections from adults when kids have trouble focusing ("I've asked you THREE TIMES to . . .") can chip away at their confidence. Socially, children who struggle with attention might talk over friends and miss the subtle cues that sustain good friendships—that facial expression that says a friend is sad, or the tone of voice that means "I really need you to listen right now."

(We all know that person who just can't listen, who's clearly planning their next comment while you're talking, or who looks around or checks their phone while you're sharing your news. No one wants their child to become that guy.)

When I work with groups of young children, I often ask two simple questions. First: "Does your parent or teacher ever tell you to 'pay attention!'?" Every hand goes up. Then I ask: "Do they teach you how to pay attention? Do you practice it?" Sudden silence, puzzled faces.

The ability to focus is a skill, and like any skill, it has to be taught and practiced—just like riding a bike or playing piano. Yet we often just say "Pay attention!" or "LISTEN!" without really helping children understand how. Instead of teaching them to notice when their mind wanders or how to create an environment for concentration, we just get frustrated when they can't focus.

Imagine how you'd feel if you were dropped in a pool and told to "just swim!" without first being taught how, or even practicing in shallow water first.

What If . . .

What if helping children focus wasn't about struggle? What if, instead of fighting against their natural need to move and play, we embrace their wiggle-bounce-sing energy and have it work for us? After decades of working with young children, I've learned that leaning into their natural tendencies is the key to real engagement and focus.

Children's brains are literally wired for movement, rhythm, and play. When we tap into these innate patterns, attention flows naturally from their genuine enthusiasm. Take balance challenges, for example. They're not just fun, they build focus while developing strength and coordination. Rhythm activities are a true secret weapon. Call-and-response clapping games aren't just entertaining, they're coordinating different parts of the brain, creating the perfect focused state for learning.

And my favorite trick for helping kids pay attention to something and remember it? Set it to a melody. (Think about how many grown-ups, in the U.S. at least, learned the alphabet with the ABC song.) If you need children to follow instructions, turn them into a simple song or say them to a beat.

Even tongue twisters (yes, really) set to a rhythm become a fantastic focus tool, and kids absolutely love them. And here's a bonus: rhythm actually helps regulate emotions because it provides structure, which is very calming and grounding for young children. When they're calm, they're ready to listen and learn.

I can hear you stressing about your musical ability or lack thereof. No need. I bet you sang to your child as an infant, and I doubt they ever filed a complaint about your pitch. Can you tap your foot to a beat? Make up silly rhymes? Do a wiggle dance? Like a champ, I'm sure. You're good.

By the way, these aren't just theoretical ideas I dreamed up while writing this book. They're golden-nugget strategies that have come out of thousands of hours of working with young children. I know they work because I've seen the magic happen again and again: chaos transforms into connection, battles over attention become bonding moments, and focus develops easily when it's wrapped in play.

In our tech-saturated world, where screens are constantly clamoring for our attention (and then shattering it to pieces), this matters more than ever.

There's approximately a zero percent chance we'll eliminate technology from our children's lives, but we can help them build the mental muscles to use it mindfully.

It's time to reframe "attention" altogether. When we stop seeing it as a fixed trait—something our child is either good at or not—and start treating it as a skill we can nurture together, one small victory at a time, everything shifts.

Here are some concrete, tried-and-true tips to help.

Setting the Stage: Tips for Attention, Focus, and Calm

Get down to your child's level. Sit near your child or kneel so you're face-to-face, making eye contact and helping them focus on you. This changes the usual power dynamic of your larger physical presence looming over them, and shows children they have your full attention. (It's also a lot harder for them to ignore you when you're RIGHT THERE.)

It isn't about getting in their face, though. It's about connecting. The physical act of coming down to their level shows you're willing to enter their world and perspective. It allows you to better read their facial expressions and body language, and vice versa. Children, especially young ones, rely heavily on nonverbal cues to understand what's going on. They'll sense your focused attention and mirror it back.

Mama Mantra

Tune in, then begin.

Use gentle touch to connect. One of the most powerful ways to get a child's attention isn't through words at all. I learned this from watching one of my kids' wonderful early childhood teachers in action. She'd notice a child starting to get squirmy or disruptive, and instead of calling them out or interrupting the lesson, she'd walk over (still talking to the group) and rest her hand softly on their shoulder. No scolding, no shaming, no power struggle. Just that quiet physical connection that said, "I see you, and I'm here with you." Almost like magic, the child would settle and tune back in.

This same approach works at home. When your child is lost in play or distracted and you need their attention, try walking over and gently touching their shoulder or reaching for their hand while you speak. The physical connection helps bridge the gap between their world and yours, and is especially powerful because it's both calming and caring. You're not making them stop what they're doing (and you're definitely not hollering from down the hall); you're helping them shift their awareness.

It's a simple strategy that can turn the struggle of trying to get your child's attention into an opportunity for connection—and by extension, cooperation.

Speak quietly. Be honest: Have you ever yelled at your kids to stop yelling? (Sadly, I have to say yes.) Does anything quite highlight the absurdity of parenting like hollering, "BE QUIET!"?

First of all, yelling doesn't work. It triggers the body's stress response, putting children in a state where it's actually harder for them to process information. They'll just tune out. Whatever you're saying gets lost in the intimidating "delivery method"—your loud voice. Yelling can also damage trust, and it models the wrong kind of communication. Do we want to raise yellers? I don't think so.

It seems counterintuitive, but speaking softly or even whispering makes children curious and more likely to listen. Try playful attention-getters in your calm, quiet voice: "If you can hear me, touch your nose!" or "Hocus pocus, time to focus."

Use positive language. Telling children what to do rather than what *not* to do paints a clear picture of the behavior you want to see, as opposed to highlighting what they're doing wrong. And a clear instruction is a lot easier for their developing brains to process and follow.

This approach maintains a constructive atmosphere and helps children develop internal motivation to behave appropriately, rather than just responding to corrections.

Focusing on the behavior you want to see sounds like "Walking feet, please" instead of "Stop running," or "We keep our hands to ourselves" instead of "Don't touch," or "Let's use our quiet voice" instead of "Stop yelling." Every "don't" instruction can be turned into a positive "do." This also avoids triggering defensive reactions ("I'M NOT YELLING!").

Basically, this language shift creates a way more positive vibe, and you now get to play the role of loving and firm guide, and not of unwanted-behavior police.

Keep instructions brief. Once you have your child's attention, give clear, concise directions. Young children can easily get overwhelmed with too many steps and too many words. Instead of "OK, here's what we're going to do! You guys listening? Great. We have a couple things to get done before going to the store. We have to—shoot, where is my phone?—get the grocery bags, I have to find the list, you have to get your shoes on and find your coat. Did you leave it outside?"

You get the point. I've already tuned out, and I'm the one writing it.

Mama Mantra

Say less, and mean it.

Use "It's time to . . ." When my son was little, he loved to set up hurdles around the house while I made dinner. When it was time to eat, I'd (very sweetly) ask, "Ready to wash your hands?" He'd zoom past with a loud "No!"

Of course he didn't want to wash his hands—he was living his best hurdle-jumping life. Why would he want to switch gears?

When we phrase instructions as questions or try to soften our directions to keep the peace, we're inadvertently giving kids the option to say no to things that aren't actually optional. It's confusing for them (and frustrating for us) when what sounds like a choice really isn't one. Asking "Want to get your seatbelt buckled?" is misleading because, really, that's not up for debate.

A language shift makes all the difference here. Instead of "Can you put your shoes on?," try "It's time to put your shoes on." Rather than "Should we clean up your toys?," say "It's time to clean up your toys now."

This isn't about being bossy or controlling; it's about being clear and consistent. Kids feel more secure when they understand exactly what's expected of them. Save the questions for times when they truly have an option: "Would you like to wear your sneakers or your boots today?"

Questions are for choices. Instructions are for must-dos. Once you put this into practice, you'll have far fewer power struggles. When I adopted "It's time to . . ." in my house, there was a massive improvement in getting my children's attention and cooperation.

My kids know all about this one and to this day will say, "Are you asking me or are you telling me?" Wise guys.

Follow-up to above: try not to repeat yourself. When you give a direct instruction, pause and wait. Give them a moment to process what you've said. We often rapid-fire repeat ourselves because we think children aren't listening, when really they just need a few seconds to shift gears. When you combine clear instructions with that bit of patience, you'll be amazed at how much more attentive kids become.

Mama Mantra

Clear is kind.

Use music, rhythm, and song. Ever notice how you can't remember where you put your phone, but you can still belt out every word to that Madonna song? Music has a magical way of embedding itself in our brains, whether we want it to or not. (Exhibit A: That Baby Shark tune.)

We've already explored the amazing ways that music engages and lights up kids' developing brains (for a refresher, flip back to Chapter 3). The bottom line is, music is way more than a nice-to-have on car rides or before naptime; it's your secret weapon for transforming everyday challenges into playful moments. It's a Mary Poppins–esque superpower, making the mundane magical and the difficult delightful.

Think about that set of instructions that you give to your child every dang day; you probably say the same thing in the same way all the time. Maybe it's during transitions like picking up toys before dinner, or maybe the bedtime routine is an issue—heading to the bathroom to brush teeth, getting jammies on.

Wherever the wheels come off the wagon, so to speak, turn those instructions you're sick of saying into catchy songs or rhythm games. Not only does this make routines way more fun, but the melodic and rhythmic patterns stick easily in children's minds, helping them remember and easily follow along.

Here are some ideas on how to weave music into daily life with kids.

- **Sing those instructions:** Instead of wrestling your toddler into their socks, sing a silly socks song (say that ten times fast). You can make up your own or put your words to a familiar melody, like "The Ants Go Marching." Or turn it into a stop-and-go number: "We're putting on our socks fast, faster, faster, and . . . FREEZE!" Contrast, like fast/slow, stop/go, or loud/soft, is an awesome attention-getter. Simple refrain songs work great too: give your child a line to repeat (this is the refrain), like "This is how we do it!," after each short, clear instruction that you give.

  Here's an example:

  You: "Let's pick our toys up fast!"
  Child: "This is how we do it!"
  You: "I'll start here, you start there."
  Child: "This is how we do it!"

  And so on—make it up as you go! Just keep it short and rhythmic.

- **Rhythm games:** Play a call-and-response game, using body percussion (claps, stomps, taps on your lap, whatever else you can think of) or tapping out a pattern on the kitchen counter or table. Come up with any short, simple rhythm and have your child repeat it back, gradually making your patterns longer or more complex. (And mix it up! Try two head taps, three claps, one stomp. Then switch it around. You get the idea.) Tongue twisters are not only silly fun but require total focus, particularly when you add layers of challenge like going faster, or try it while balancing on one foot. (It's hard to be thinking about anything else when you're trying to say "Irish wristwatch" as fast as you can.)

- **Use a unique musical sound,** like a bell, a chime, or tapping a glass with a fork, to capture your child's attention. The single clear tone can work better than any amount of "Please calm down." It's like pressing pause on the chaos, creating a moment of calm curiosity that naturally draws children's focus. (This can be a great listening activity too: focusing on a single sound that rings for a while is an excellent way to practice paying attention.)

The real gift is that using music does double duty: it makes parents' daily routines smoother and gives our children tools for focus and attention. Once you start looking for opportunities, I bet you'll find tons of moments throughout the day where a simple song or rhythm game can transform a power struggle into playful connection. It's way more fun for you too.

Do something totally unexpected. Freeze mid-sentence, striking a dramatic pose. Talk in a robot voice or try a silly accent. Pop on a funny hat! Start moving in super-slow motion!

Why does this work? Pattern interruption triggers the brain's novelty response, naturally drawing attention. Kids are essentially startled into pausing what they're doing as they think, "Wait, what?"

Humor and surprise release dopamine, which is one of those feel-good hormones we're always hearing about. And physical movement or silly voices give multisensory input, making the moment even more attention-getting.

Is it goofy? You bet. Effective? Yes.

Try balance challenges. Balance activities light up children's brains with focused attention, naturally pulling kids into a sweet spot of concentration because they have to tune in to what their body is doing right now. It's a playful way of getting your child to zero in on the present moment, while also building core muscles and coordination skills they need.

When you're trying not to fall off a pretend tightrope, you can't help but focus. Your child may be envisioning their future in the circus, but what's really happening is that they're strengthening their ability to sustain attention while their bodies are in motion.

Incorporate lots of movement. Unstructured movement like dancing, wiggling, and shaking helps reset kids' nervous systems and wake up their brains. When children shake like a wet dog (see Puppy Shake on page 97) or wiggle like a worm in the mud, they're doing exactly what their bodies need to transition between activities and get ready to focus.

Build in quick movement breaks: a one-minute full-out dance party, a full-body wiggle, kangaroo jumps while counting out loud to twenty.

These work about a million times better than repeating, "Stop fidgeting." You won't believe how much more readily your child can concentrate afterward.

It's easy to forget about the huge role our own mindset plays, but just as children unconsciously mirror our speaking patterns and gestures, they also absorb and reflect our energy levels and emotional state. The way we show up—scattered or centered, distracted or fully present—has a massive effect on our child's ability to engage. When we prioritize our own sense of groundedness, we create an environment that naturally supports our child's capacity for paying attention.

Let's give our children the opportunity to observe focused, present grown-ups. Modeling is everything.

Here are some tips for you to try.

Shift the Spotlight

Just as a spotlight illuminates whatever it's pointing to, your focus amplifies whatever part of your child's behavior you're choosing to notice in the moment. It's totally natural for that to be the challenging stuff–the pile of couch cushions on the floor, the crumbs everywhere, the pushback on really anything you ask them to do–but you can intentionally shift your "spotlight" to the moments of growth and connection that are also happening.

This isn't about ignoring problems that need addressing, or letting go of the fact that you do really need your child to focus and listen. You're simply balancing your attention to include the good that's already there while breaking the habit of letting challenging behaviors monopolize your attention (and then run on a loop in your head–I get it). By consciously directing your spotlight toward what's working, you create more space for joy and connection in your relationship with your child.

When you try this, you might find that the positive moments multiply–

not necessarily because your child's behavior has dramatically changed, but because you're tuning in to the good stuff that's been there all along.

HOW-TO

Pause and take a breath. Notice where your attention is. Are you caught in a loop of noticing what's going wrong? Just observe.

Now, just as you'd direct a spotlight onstage, consciously decide to shift your beam of attention. Look for moments of kindness, effort, or joy—even tiny ones. It might be the way your child carefully carries their plate to the sink or how gently they pet the cat.

Once you spot something positive, let your attention linger there. Notice the details: your child's concentrated expression, their small smile, their careful touch.

Breathe, allowing these sweet observations to seep in. Remember, there's a heck of a lot more good than "bad."

Let these positive moments relax you and lift your mood if you can. Your child will likely sense this shift in your energy; it will help them feel seen and valued.

Cool It Down

Taking long, intentional breaths requires that we pause and slow down, which interrupts our stress response and helps activate our body's natural relaxation system. This is an ideal "gimme a minute" technique you can use anytime and anywhere, particularly when you're struggling to get your child to focus and pay attention.

And of course, your child learns by watching you. When they see you taking calming breaths, you're teaching them valuable coping skills too. They may join in, especially the littlest ones who love to imitate us. Win!

HOW-TO

Make a small O shape with your mouth, as if you were about to drink from a thin straw. As slowly as you can, breathe in.

Notice how the air feels cooler, and how it might create a slight whistling sound–this can help you focus.

Relax your mouth and exhale as slowly as you can. It might be helpful to count silently as you do it.

Repeat this three to five times, or for as long as you have. Even one of these breaths, done intentionally, can help.

Here Are My Hands

Touch is one of our most immediate senses, serving as a strong "anchor" to the present moment. Putting your hands flat on a nearby surface creates distinct physical sensations that give your mind something concrete and current to focus on, making it easier to step out of those spinning thoughts about how your child will never succeed in life if they keep forgetting their water bottle. It's essentially creating a home base for your attention.

HOW-TO

Place both palms flat against your chosen surface–it could be your desk, the kitchen counter, or your own lap or heart.

Spread your fingers wide and feel the entire surface of your palms making contact. Pay attention to any sensations like pressure or texture. Notice the temperature of the surface against your skin.

Take a few long, slow breaths while maintaining awareness of your hands. With each breath, you might notice tiny movements or changes in how they feel.

Try to let your attention rest in the physical sensations of your hands. If your mind wanders, simply notice that and bring your focus back to the feeling in your hands. Stay here as long as you like.

Connection Activities

Watch me demonstrate all of these Brain Booster activities, songs, and rhythm games, plus get the playlist, right here!

These activities are all about helping kids focus their attention and energize their brains—think of them as fun workouts for young minds. We've got balance challenges that develop coordination, rhythm games that fire up concentration, playful movement, and confidence-boosting affirmations. Feel free to adjust, embellish, or create your own—the key is keeping things engaging, active, and suited to your child.

Flamingo

This playful balance activity requires children's brains to juggle multiple tasks at once–keeping their body upright, adjusting their weight, processing visual information–creating neural pathways that help them build their attention-span "muscles."

SONG PAIRING: "Balancing Act"

SCRIPT

Let's be flamingos!
Flamingos are big pink birds that love to stand on one leg.
Stand up tall and strong, with both feet on the floor.
Slowly lift one knee up toward your belly.
Keep your belly strong!
If you feel wobbly, hold on to something or someone.
(*Offer your hand for balance if needed.*)
Spread your wings out wide to the sides.
You're a flamingo!
Breathe in, and breathe out.
Hold your body as still as you can.
Look at you, flamingo!
Breathe in, and breathe out.

Slowly put your knee down.
Let's try it again!
(*Repeat, using the other leg.*)

IN THE CLASSROOM: Have students stand next to their desks or close to a wall so they have support if needed. If balance feels like a challenge, begin with hands on hips before trying with arms out wide. Practice just lifting the knee slightly at first—the toes can stay on the floor—gradually working up to lifting the leg off the ground. You can also incorporate counting: "Let's be flamingos for five seconds—count with me!"

1-2-3 Clap!

This quick attention-grabber is how I start every school assembly with hundreds of wiggly children. It works brilliantly. The simple pattern of counting, clapping, and breathing helps children focus through rhythm and repetition, while the tactile feedback of rubbing the palms together encourages mindful awareness. It's basically a reset button for chatterboxes.

SONG PAIRING: "Clap and Stop!"

SCRIPT
Open your arms out really wide.
Count one, two, three . . . and CLAP your hands one time!
Rub your hands together and make some energy.
Put your hands on your head. Take a long breath in, and let it all out.
Open your arms out really wide again.
Count one, two, three . . . and CLAP your hands one time!
Rub your hands together, a little faster this time. Make some energy!
Put your hands on your belly. Take a long breath in, and let it all out.
Open your arms out really wide one more time.
Count one, two, three . . . and CLAP your hands one time!
Rub your hands together, even faster this time. Make some energy!
Put your hands over your heart.
Take a really long, slow breath in, and let it all the way out.

IN THE CLASSROOM: I use this to get the attention of hundreds of students literally every time I do a performance or assembly. Don't introduce it, just do it. Use consistent language every time.

Modify the script as follows:

Show me your hands!
(Demonstrate hands held up with palms out.)
I'm going to count to three, and we'll clap one time. One, two, three . . . CLAP!
(Continue with the script, using the above lines each time for the clap.)

Rhythm & Rhyme Time

Kids all up in each other's business? Here's an easy-to-learn rhythm-based chant that works at home or in the classroom to help them respect others' personal space. There's a video too (use the QR code on page 94).

Hands to Myself!

(*Clap or tap a steady beat.*)
I keep my hands to myself
My hands to myself
I keep my hands on MY body
Not on anybody else!

I put my hands on my head (*Add these motions.*)
My hands on my nose
I put my hands on my knees
My hands on my toes

I keep my hands to myself
My hands to myself
I keep my hands on MY body
Not on anybody else!

Puppy Shake

Big, unstructured movements like full-body shaking can help children release excess energy and "reset" their nervous systems, improving concentration. Ideally it's done standing, but can easily be adapted to be done seated. Who doesn't love to shake like a wet puppy?

SONG PAIRING: "Shake It"

SCRIPT

Pretend you're a puppy, and you just had a bath.
You're all wet!
Give your head and shoulders a tiny little shake.
Give your arms a medium shake.
Give your legs a big shake.
Give your whole body a HUGE shake!
Can you shake your tail?
Shake, shake, shake, little puppy!
Shake, shake, shake!
Now start to slow down.
Slow down a little more.
Hold your body still.
Breathe in, and breathe out.

IN THE CLASSROOM: With an active, movement-based activity like this, it's a good idea to have clear ground rules ahead of time. Consider establishing a Personal Puppy Bubble rule to prevent collisions. Or you could do the activity freeze-dance style, where you use a song like "Shake It" and everyone knows to stop when the music does. Encourage students to notice how their bodies feel before and after they shake.

I Am Smart!

There's real science behind the power and effectiveness of positive affirmations—they can help children build self-confidence and develop resilience and perseverance. You can change "smart" to any positive word you like, or have your child pick their own.

**SONG PAIRING:** "Strong, Smart, Kind"

SCRIPT

Take a long breath in, and let the air all the way out.
Say: "I am smart."
Breathe in, and breathe out.
Touch one hand to your head, where your smart brain is.
Say it again, a little louder: "I am smart!"
Breathe in, and breathe out.
Touch the other hand to your head, where your smart brain is.
Give your head a little pat.
Say it again, even louder: "I AM SMART!"
Bring your hands down.
Take a long breath in, and let it all the way out.

IN THE CLASSROOM: There are lots of variations to try here. Ask each student to come up with their own positive word to finish the phrase "I am . . ." or come up with one as a class. You could add a new word each day or week and create a Power Poster or wall in the classroom to display them, adding new ones as you go. Students could create their own individual affirmation cards to decorate and keep. Add movement or a gesture to go with each word (hands on heart for "kind," for example). You could even send home notes or an email about the affirmations so families can reinforce them.

Rhythm & Rhyme Time

Call-and-response tongue twisters are a blast—and they train your child's brain to stay completely tuned in. Children have to listen closely to catch every word, hold it in their memory, and then fire it right back at you. Add a beat to the mix, and you've got their full attention locked in, creating fun, focused connection. Be sure to watch the video for this one (use the QR code on page 94)!

Betty Botter

(*Keep a steady beat by clapping or tapping, as fast or as slowly as you'd like. Say one line at a time and have your child repeat it back to you. Get faster and faster, or add layers of challenge, like saying it while standing on one foot!*)

Betty Botter bought some butter
But she said this butter's bitter
If I put it in my batter
It will make my batter bitter
But a bit of better butter
That will make my batter better!
Betty Botter bought some butter
Better than the bitter butter
And she put it in her batter
And her batter was not bitter!

Rainstorm

Children love creating their own rainstorm—from the wind picking up to a thunderous downpour and back again—using simple body percussion. The sensory feedback of rubbing their hands together, tapping, clapping, and stomping lights up their brains and gets them ready to focus.

 **SONG PAIRING:** "Here Comes the Thunderstorm"

SCRIPT

Uh-oh, I think it might rain!

Rub your hands together to make the sound of the wind picking up.

Tap your fingers and thumb together next to your ears—can you hear the raindrops?

Now tap your hands on your lap, one after the other—it's really starting to rain!

Get faster and faster—now it's pouring!

We're going to get soaked!

Lightning! Clap your hands up high!

Thunder! Stomp your feet!

Lightning! Clap your hands up high!

Thunder! Stomp your feet!

Tap those hands on your lap again, super fast—it's really raining hard!

Now start to slow them down . . . I think the rain might be stopping . . .

Slow down a little more . . .

Tap your fingers and thumb together next to your ears—there are still a few raindrops . . .

Now rub your hands together to make the sound of the wind.

It's going to blow the last of the storm away.

Slooow your hands down, slooow them down a little more, and stop.

Everything is still and quiet.

IN THE CLASSROOM: Read the script as written, making the "storm" last as long as you see fit. I often start with a quiet "Shhh . . . do you hear that?" while rubbing my hands together next to my ear for the wind; this gets the group's attention. I let them stay in the "pouring rain" (tapping on laps super-fast) section for a good bit—it tires them out pretty quickly! Make this activity your own by turning it into a snowstorm in the winter, adding different sounds for rain in the forest or on a roof, or swaying side to side for big gusts of wind. You could dim or turn off the lights to signal that the storm is coming. And if you're feeling extra, use a fine-mist spray bottle of water for the rain!

Rhythm & Rhyme Time

Using the universal hand sign for peace, this rhyme combines simple motions with consistent rhythm, fully engaging children's bodies and brains. Watch me do it on the Brain Boosters webpage (use the QR code on page 94).

Peace Fingers

(*Make peace fingers with the index and middle fingers of both hands, and follow the motions in the rhyme.*)

Peace fingers, peace fingers
Lift them up and down! (*Reach up high and back down.*)
Peace fingers, peace fingers
Wave them all around! (*Actively wave your hands.*)
Peace fingers, peace fingers
Hide them away. (*Hands behind your back.*)
Peace fingers, peace fingers
Let's have peace today. (*Hands on heart, long breath in and out.*)

Variation

Peace fingers, peace fingers
One-two-three!
Peace fingers, peace fingers
Peace begins with me. (*Hands on heart, long breath in and out.*)

I Am Awesome Because . . .

Celebrating what makes us amazing is always a good thing. This confidence-boosting exercise helps both you and your child recognize your unique strengths and wonderful qualities while creating a moment of pure fun and joy together. Bonus points for getting up and flexing in a power pose, or whatever makes you both feel like rockstars!

SONG PAIRING: "I Am Awesome"

HOW-TO

You can do this seated, but ideally you'll both stand and take up lots of space: feet wide, arms out and up. Making "muscles" would be amazing.

Ask your child: "What makes you awesome?"

Help them complete this sentence: "I am awesome because . . ."

Encourage them to say it again: "I AM AWESOME because . . ."

They can repeat the same word or pick as many different positive words as they want.

Play it up by saying, "I can't hear you . . . !"

Have them say it again, even louder: "I AM AWESOME because . . ."

Say, "Yes you are!" Give hugs, high fives, fist pumps. Woohoo!

Now it's your turn. Share what makes YOU awesome using the same format. Get into it. Because you are actually fabulous!

Take turns going back and forth, celebrating different awesome qualities.

Take a deep breath in together, and let it all the way out.

End with lots of celebration, reminding each other to remember your awesome sentences all day long. Revisit them at bedtime for even more awesomeness.

Brain Boosters Playlist

"Balancing Act"

Whimsical and bouncy, perfect for movement and balance challenges.

"Clap and Stop!"

A stop-and-go song with motions–incredible for capturing attention and focus.

"Shake It"

A high-energy movement tune that lights up the brain and totally resets the vibe.

"Strong, Smart, Kind"

Empowering and bold, an anthem that helps children build confidence from the inside out.

"Here Comes the Thunderstorm"

With built-in motions, children can act out a dramatic rainstorm, from the clouds rolling in to thunder crashing and rain pouring down.

"I Am Awesome"

A beat-driven, confidence-building chant where kids celebrate their specialness by spelling out A-W-E-S-O-M-E!

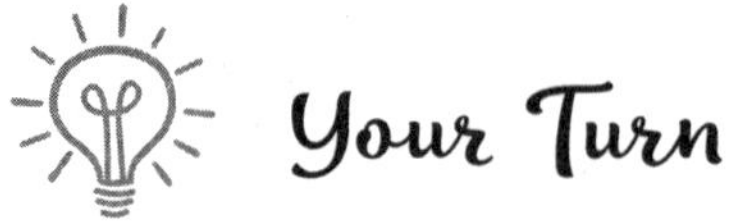

Build Your Child's Natural Ability to Focus and Listen

Maybe you've wondered if you're doing something wrong when your child can't focus for more than thirty seconds. But the truth is, attention isn't a talent your child either has or doesn't have. Attention is a skill you can build together, and it can be really fun in the process. Now you have the understanding and tools to make it happen.

When you use the playful practices in this chapter, you're actively creating an environment where focus flows naturally from your child's own joy and enthusiasm. Every balance challenge, rhythm game, and tongue twister is intentionally building their mental muscles in a way that feels like play—because it is play.

Think about what you can now create: your child can follow directions the first time because you've turned your instructions into a catchy song; they can listen well in conversations because their bodies and brains are calm and under control; and homework time doesn't end in tears because you've improved their ability to focus through playful, mindful practices.

Using the simple tools in this chapter—ones that work with your child's natural wiring instead of against it—you now have the power to create the focused, engaged dynamic you've been looking for with your child.

When you use these Calm & Connect steps, you'll Create:

More of This

Focused attention and engaged listening

Cooperation without battles

Joyful energy and laughter

Clear, effective communication

Deep connection through eye contact and gentle touch

Confidence in your ability to engage your child

Less of That

Uncertainty about what approach to try

Struggling to get your child to focus

Raising your voice

Your child tuning you out

Feeling distracted (both you and your child)

Focusing on undesired behaviors

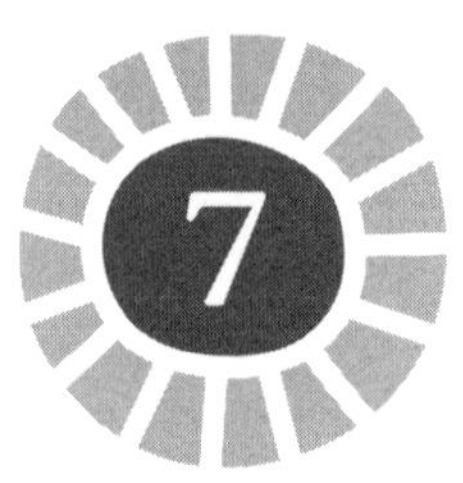

Let's Play

Preserving the Magic and Wonder of Your Child's Early Years

CHILDREN ARE BORN with an innate sense of wonder. They marvel at the simplest things—a tiny beetle on the ground, the sound of their voice echoing in an empty room. They live in the present moment, immersed in whatever captures their attention. They're natural practitioners of mindfulness!

Safeguarding this instinctive capacity for curiosity and fascination is fundamental to raising a joyful child. It's the foundation of childhood well-being, and it deserves our fierce protection. Letting our children be children—giving them plenty of space and time to stretch their imaginations, move their bodies, and explore their surroundings—is essential for their health and happiness.

In our instant-gratification, achievement-oriented society, it's easy to forget that play isn't just something children do for fun—it's how they learn about themselves and their world. It's through play that children develop creativity, flexibility, problem-solving skills, and resilience. A child who spends an afternoon absorbed in building a fairy house from sticks and leaves is developing these skills without a curriculum or coach in sight.

Why It's Hard

There's a lot of societal pressure to "enrich" our children and prepare them for their futures practically from birth. We sign them up for soccer, piano, and coding camp—feeling like they'll fall behind if we don't—shuttling them from one activity to the next, squeezing in dinner on the go between gymnastics and tutoring.

Even when we do carve out "free time," we often feel compelled to supervise and direct it. A big part of this, I think, is that we're uncomfortable with boredom—our children's and our own. When was the last time you waited in a doctor's office without looking at your phone?

Also, a child left to their own devices to freely play can create noise, mess, and chaos that we sometimes don't have the energy to manage; screens promise peace and quiet (not to mention "educational content"). Unstructured, non-screen play can feel like a quaint relic of the past, when the truth is it's a developmental necessity.

What If . . .

Instead of racing to the next "enrichment opportunity," what if we intentionally carved out and protected time and space for our children to simply play? What if we saw the mess, the mud, and even the occasional bump or bruise as worthwhile tradeoffs for the invaluable development happening just beneath the surface?

It's vitally important to let kids be kids as long as possible—to protect their right to play freely in a world that increasingly pushes them toward structured activities, screen-based entertainment, and outward achievements.

The activities in this chapter help you connect with your child in their natural play state—joining their world rather than pulling them into the structured adult one. The practices honor how children learn through movement, imagination, and sensory exploration. These aren't sit-still-with-eyes-closed exercises (nothing wrong with those, of course; this just isn't the time or place), but invitations to be fully present in ways that feel natural for young children.

I'll also share ways for you to reconnect with your own sense of joy and wonder from childhood. Because when we get lost in play alongside our children—getting messy with finger paints or making up silly dances—we not only strengthen our bond with our child, we also reclaim a part of ourselves that we may have forgotten about for too long.

Setting the Stage: Tips for Playtime

Let's start by looking at some concrete strategies for creating an environment that supports playful discovery and gives your child the space to explore, create, and simply be themselves, along with suggestions on how to step back and let your child take the lead.

Let them be bored. Hearing a whiny "I'm sooo bored" understandably makes most of us want to immediately solve the problem by making a suggestion, leading a game, or handing them an electronic device. Resist! Yes, you can. You do not need to fill every moment—or even most of them—of your child's day with activities.

Boredom is not something to save our children from—it's actually how they find their way to the most creative play and their most imaginative adventures. When children push through their initial discomfort and frustration on their own (and they will), they discover inner resources they didn't know they had.

What's happening in their brains during these moments is amazing. A fancy phrase for boredom is "neurological downtime," which is when connections form between previously unrelated ideas, sparking original thinking that structured activities don't allow space for. Your child's developing brain actually needs these periods of unscheduled time to build neural pathways and develop executive function skills.

When grown-ups lead play, we establish the rules and children simply have to learn them and comply. In free play, children make up the games and negotiate everything themselves—and this is where crucial social skills develop. Kids who create their own play worlds learn to problem-solve without adult intervention. They also assign themselves roles based on interest rather than taking the position a grown-up or coach gives them, which helps them discover their own passions and preferences.

My boys and their friends invented a game they called BlitzBall in our backyard. It was a wild hybrid of football, baseball, and wiffleball, with a lawn chair somehow involved, and it had constantly changing rules. They very loudly negotiated said rules, resolved their many disputes, and adjusted their game on the fly. (When my younger son later went to baseball camp, he was initially confused by the rigid structure, because he was so accustomed to the flexibility of their made-up creation.)

Mama Mantra

The less we direct, the more they discover.

You can handle your child's momentary discomfort when they complain of having "nothing to do"—it won't last. And what emerges on the other side might be something wonderful that neither of you could have imagined—and is exactly what your child's developing brain needs.

Also, feel free to try my standard response to complaints of boredom: "You're bored? Oh, great! The bathroom needs cleaning, there's a lot of vacuuming to be done, and the kitchen . . ." Before I could finish, my children would practically teleport out of my presence and discover fascinating activities that weren't there moments before. Works like a charm.

Less is more when it comes to toys. Clutter is a silent chaos-maker, and toys are a major contributor. When playthings are scattered everywhere, it's overwhelming for everyone, especially your child. Their developing brain isn't designed to process so much visual stimuli all at once—that pile of toys isn't expanding their imagination; it's actually shutting it down. It might seem counterintuitive, but children actually play more creatively and for longer periods when they have fewer toys to choose from.

When we accumulate too many things, each item inherently loses value. Think about it: How can we—or our children—truly appreciate what we have when we can't even keep track of it all? Having more actually gives your child less—less appreciation, less engagement, and less joy from each individual thing.

Reduce that visual noise with covered bins or baskets that streamline the space while making cleanup easier. Keep just a handful of toys accessible and in view and rotate them—this creates the magic of rediscovery, and it really works. When children encounter a toy they haven't seen for a while, they play with it as if finding it for the first time—it's like when you find a great sweater in the back of your closet that you forgot you had.

Start the "one project at a time" rule early—like, really early. Before moving to a new activity, game, or project, toys from the current one get put away. This teaches respect for their belongings and space (and helps preserve your sanity).

Remember, your home isn't a toy store and you don't need to stock it like one. Creating calm, ordered spaces for play isn't just good for your mental health; it allows your child to play more meaningfully and creatively with fewer, better-loved treasures. The result will be fewer meltdowns from overwhelm and a more peaceful space for everyone.

Mama Mantra

Less toys, more joy.

Lean into open-ended playthings. Here's the thing about the shiny, battery-powered toys that only have one function: children get bored with them really quickly. That electronic puppy that flips and barks is fascinating for about fifteen minutes, then gets tossed aside when the novelty disappears, and on we go with the frustrating—not to mention expensive—cycle of demand for new things to play with.

The toys that encourage endless play, the ones that actually last, are the simplest ones. Sometimes they're not even "toys" at all. My youngest carried around a section of green garden hose for an entire summer. It wasn't a "real" toy—but in his world, it was essential equipment for yard work, a fire hose for emergencies, and a telescope for looking at the moon, depending on the day. The possibilities were endless because there were no built-in limitations. Pots, pans, and measuring cups work wonders on the kitchen floor; children naturally make games out of whatever they have.

For your child, open-ended playthings mean a shift from "What does this toy do?" to "What can I do with this toy?" It's a profound difference, and it puts your child in the driver's seat of their own play experience, injecting huge amounts of creativity in the process.

To be clear, I'm not suggesting you give your child some empty cardboard boxes and call it a day. Actual toys are great; just keep them as

A quick word about loving and well-intentioned gift-givers

I spent years politely persuading grandparents and other relatives that another plastic guitar that played tinny, repetitive songs at the push of a button wasn't what we were going for. ("But you love music!" I'd get in reply.) Loop in your gift-givers early and gently; share your philosophy and suggest alternatives they can feel good about buying. They don't have to agree with your approach, but what comes into your home is ultimately your decision. If the battery-operated dinosaur that roars in three languages still arrives, there's always the mysterious case of the batteries that didn't arrive with it, and never do.

simple as possible. That plastic doll with the big permanent smile can only ever be happy, but a simpler little friend with minimal facial features can experience a fuller range of emotions, giving your child the chance to comfort, celebrate, or care for their charge, depending on their play scenario at the moment. The toys that have survived multiple purges in our home—the ones I hope to hand down to the next generation—are wooden blocks, play silks, simple cars and trucks, and musical instruments.

Please don't stress about providing "educational" toys (I fell for those Baby Einstein videos too). Let's not get sucked in by claims of teaching literacy, counting, or coding skills. Your child is getting a far better education when they work at turning a blanket into a cave by balancing it just so over the furniture; they're developing executive function skills and creative thinking that no programmed toy can deliver. Electronics, particularly screen-based "toys," are no match for hands-on, trial-and-error learning, and they usually overstimulate rather than educate children anyway.

When you offer your child simple toys, or raw materials like old sheets and blankets, crayons and scissors and paper, boxes, buckets and glue, they get to decide what they'll turn them into. These humble supplies can become forts, art masterpieces, dragon lairs, or treasure maps; the list goes on and on. Their developing brains will benefit way more from open-ended exploration than from toys that essentially do the playing for them.

Get them outside. When my kids were small, they went to a school where outside play was considered essential; out they went in every imaginable type of weather. We provided waterproof everything: boots, puddle pants, and raincoats, plus mittens, winter hats and sun hats, and layers upon layers that they outgrew five minutes after I bought them. Oh, the laundry—mud-caked snowpants, grass-stained shirts, and soggy socks in small mountains by our back door.

My youngest came home from first grade one day saying his foot hurt, and upon inspection I discovered I had sent him to school wearing two left boots—that's how much we had in the way of outdoor footwear lying around. We were committed. And although there were plenty of scrapes and bumps and the occasional bout of poison ivy, my children genuinely loved being outdoors, and still do. My boys now happily go for runs in the pouring rain, no matter how cold or miserable it is.

Now a teen, my youngest still spends hours outside with neighborhood kids, exploring the creek and building treehouses and carving out bike trails—I have an actual bell I ring when I need him to come home. (Yes, he does have a phone. I really like to ring the bell, though.) My kids' comfort in the natural world, their resilience, and their ability to entertain themselves without screens much of the time make the years of boot swaps, mitten searches, and laundry mountains completely worth it.

Get your child outside, every day, rain or shine, warm or cold—it's fundamental for developing brains and bodies. There's real science behind the value of outside time for kids; countless books have been written about it. One standout is *Last Child in the Woods* by Richard Louv, where he puts it this way: "Time in nature is not leisure time; it's an essential investment in our children's health." Research consistently shows that children who spend substantial time outdoors have better concentration, less anxiety, and stronger immune systems. One study found that just twenty minutes in nature significantly reduced stress levels in children. It's so worth it.

When children play in natural environments, their sensory systems develop in ways that just can't be replicated indoors. Uneven terrain builds body awareness and balance as kids navigate rocks, hills, and soft earth. Unlike controlled indoor environments where temperature, lighting, and conditions remain constant, nature has unpredictable elements like sudden breezes, bright sun that turns to shade, or unexpected raindrops that require children to adapt their play, their clothing, or their shelter, teaching adaptability and resilience. It's how children learn, on their own, how to solve problems and manage themselves—and these skills transfer to all aspects of life.

Nature also provides the ultimate playground for developing creativity. A fallen tree branch becomes a magic wand, a sword, or a tool for drawing in the dirt. One of my older son's sweetest memories from his nature-based early childhood school was "boat races." The boats? Plain old sticks. After a good rain, each child would carefully select their stick, place it in the rushing creek, and watch and cheer with absolute delight to see whose "boat" would travel fastest downstream. They did it for hours.

Don't let the whole bundling-up thing be a barrier. As they say, there's no such thing as bad weather, just inappropriate clothing. You don't need fancy outdoor gear—layer up with what you have or swap clothes with other parents. I've found amazing outerwear for incredibly cheap prices at thrift stores. Good boots, a raincoat, and a whole bunch of layers go a long way. (I kept a box of mismatched mittens and gloves by our back door because somehow we always lost one but never both.)

Get your child suited up and let them splash in puddles, collect rocks and pinecones, and dig in the dirt. Yes, it's messier and requires more effort on your part than letting them stay inside. And yes, your child's body, brain, and spirit will thank you.

Protect unscheduled time for your child. Too many activities and not enough free time? You're definitely not alone. In our desire to give our children every possible advantage (especially if we didn't have those opportunities ourselves), we often fill our calendars to overflowing with sports, music lessons, dance team, and clubs.

But when every minute is planned, children lose the ability to direct themselves. Overscheduling creates a reliance on external structure and gratification, to the point where some children truly don't know what to do when football practice is canceled, as they've become dependent on others to direct their time and energy.

I understand the privilege inherent in being able to provide these experiences, and I also understand the pull to sign up for all the things, especially if your child is asking and their friends seem to all be doing them. But finding the sweet spot between enrichment and overwhelm is crucial for your child's healthy development. When we offset structured activities with plenty of free time, we support our children's emotional well-being and their ability to manage themselves. It's an essential balance to find.

I think of the things my kids created with their free afternoons—their made-up club with elaborate rules, the baseball dugout built from scrap wood, the bike trails they called the Rocky Mountains—that have become the stuff of family legend. Those unstructured hours created their most cherished memories and developed skills no structured activity could ever teach.

Let me be clear: I'm a huge fan of music instruction, learning of all kinds, and team sports. I played soccer and ran track through college, all my kids played on teams, and my son plays college soccer. For us, what worked was to do one sport at a time, not two or three, and we didn't include additional things like piano lessons during the same season. That's what worked for our family, but I'd never suggest that our approach is the universal solution—every child is unique, and your family has their own unique needs.

Mindful awareness is your most reliable guide for navigating this equation—not what anyone else says or what any other family is doing. Let your sister's kids do two sports plus flute each season—good for them. Keep your eyes on your own game, so to speak, watching for signals from your child like irritability and crankiness or fatigue, which will likely mean they're doing too much. Children need space to discover what they truly love and are drawn to, not just what we've signed them up for. This is how they develop independence, creativity, and a sense of self.

So, before you sign up for that next activity, ask yourself: "Will my child still have plenty of time and space with nothing planned on the calendar?" While unstructured playtime might mean your living room gets turned into a rather messy enchanted forest, the benefits for your child far, far outweigh the inconveniences.

A note about play after school

Young children work really hard all day at school or daycare following rules, navigating social dynamics, and processing new information–it's exhausting work for their developing brains and bodies. Think about it: they've been sitting still in tiny chairs, waiting to speak until they're called on, sharing the toys like they're supposed to, and generally holding it all together–by 3 PM, they're fried.

What they desperately need after school is the opportunity to decompress and release all that pent-up energy and tension. Transition time with no agenda whatsoever is crucial for their emotional well-being. Free play right after school (ideally outside) allows their nervous systems to reset and recover from the demands of the day.

Think of it as a pressure valve that builds up gradually during the school day–if it doesn't release right after school, it's going to come out soon enough, meaning someone's going to be crying before dinner. Let them run wild for a bit. Your child's mental health–not to mention a more peaceful evening routine for you–is one hundred percent worth it.

Put them to work. I'm serious. Children love to have an important purpose. They naturally want to participate in "grown-up" work—not just pretend at it. My children had their own child-sized tools from early on: a small wooden broom and dustpan, a crumb scraper (this was a favorite), a miniature sturdy shovel, and functional cooking implements. They felt a visible sense of accomplishment when they successfully swept up a pile of crumbs or helped clear the snowy walk.

When children work alongside you in genuine tasks, they develop confidence and a sense of belonging in the household. It's truly satisfying for a child to contribute to the family in meaningful ways. When they carry a watering can to the plants, carefully balancing so it doesn't spill, they're not only building physical coordination and focus, they're also developing a sense of "I can do this!" that becomes foundational to their self-image.

My son would positively beam when he made his own toast—it took about twenty minutes for him to spread the butter, but he was very proud of himself, and now he's the cool guy in his college house who can actually cook.

Children feel truly seen when we trust them with real responsibility. Incorporate opportunities for them to participate in home-care tasks wherever you can—it takes longer at first and might require a fair amount of refolding the towels, but you're building both skills and your relationship. Skip the plastic pretend implements that don't really work and will be broken by the end of the week; let children participate using real tools they can handle, or ones sized for them.

When you start this early, chores don't feel like chores in the usual dreaded sense; household tasks are just a natural part of family life—they're "what we do." Children who grow up participating in household work don't suddenly resist (as much, anyway) at helping when they're older. My youngest is now the best laundry folder in the family by far.

I can attest that over time this genuinely becomes helpful. What starts as mostly cute but somewhat messy "helping" gradually transforms into real assistance. Those early investments of patience pay off big-time when you suddenly realize your children are completely capable of contributing to running the household.

For young children, there's no clear line between work and play. Deep learning and a strong sense of self come when "work" feels playful and when play has purpose.

Working together also creates easy, authentic moments of connection with your child as you "share" the load and celebrate small wins together. Who doesn't love checking things off a list?

Let them wonder. Let's preserve our children's sense of magical possibility and allow them to inhabit the sweet "bubble" of childhood as long as they can. Everything doesn't need to be a teachable moment. When your child asks what makes the stars sparkle in the sky, try responding with something like "Hmm, I wonder . . ." and leave it at that, instead of launching into a scientific explanation.

This bubble of childhood is precious and fleeting; our culture pushes children to grow up quickly. Eventually, reality will find its way in—that's the natural progression of growing up—but there's no need to hurry it along with our explanations, no matter how well intentioned. Let children believe fairies live in garden flowers or that stuffed animals have secret lives for as long as possible. Each time we correct one of their fantasy ideas with facts, we poke a hole in their lovely bubble.

I know how tempting it is when you've finally bundled everyone up for that nature walk to make it educational at every turn. "See how the leaves are changing color? That's because the chlorophyll is breaking down to show the carotenoids underneath . . ." (To be clear, I didn't actually know that. I had to look it up.) But the facts and science will come soon enough. Marveling at a bear-shaped cloud together is significantly better for your young child's emotional development than explaining cloud formation, and it creates a far more meaningful connection between you.

Mama Mantra

Let wonder lead the way.

Resist the urge to turn everything into a teaching moment, and you'll actually teach your child something more valuable—that imagination and wonder are worthy experiences in themselves.

Be fully present when you play. I know what you're thinking: "I'm with them ALL DAY LONG, for Pete's sake. I have to put my heart and soul into playing Family too??" I get it. I never liked playing Family either. (I could get down on the rug and build a city out of blocks with the best of them, though.) Let's get this right out there: it's completely OK not to enjoy playing certain games with your child.

But when you are playing together, truly be there. Not just your physical body, but your full emotional presence too. This makes all the difference for your connection. When you put your phone in a drawer before joining your child, they get the clear message that you're focusing completely on them. Don't try to multitask by having the news on or your phone next to you just in case. (Sorry to say, even when your phone is face down, your child can sense your divided attention.)

There's no "right" amount of time to play with your child, and there's no rule I'm aware of that says you have to enthusiastically participate in every game they want you to be a part of. What matters most is giving your child your full presence and attention when you do play with them. They can sense when you're forcing it.

Here's something I used to do when I was struggling to be genuinely present at playtime: I'd pick an activity I truly liked, like painting with watercolors—and just start doing it where my child could see me. I didn't announce it or invite them to join; I just got absorbed in it myself. More often than not, my child naturally became curious, gravitated toward what I was doing, and wanted to get in on it, creating an organic opportunity for shared play without me having to force enthusiasm for something I didn't particularly enjoy.

Now, instead of dragging yourself into something, you're both fully present in a shared, authentic experience of play.

Calm Starts with You

It's surprisingly easy amid all our day-to-day challenges with young children and, you know, Life, to forget how to have fun. These exercises are invitations to reclaim parts of yourself that may have been temporarily misplaced beneath shopping lists and loads of laundry. Remember that your joy doesn't need to be separate from your parenting—in fact, it's essential to show your child what it means to be fully in the moment and embrace joy.

Play Like You Mean It

Remember when play wasn't something you scheduled and supervised, but something you got lost in until you were called for dinner? When you'd lose track of time building tiny houses or racing bikes down the street? That pure delight is still in there somewhere, and reconnecting with it can turn playtime with your child from yet another parenting task into a genuine source of joy.

When you truly engage, you're modeling what it means to be fully present with your child, and that connection is the best gift you can give them.

HOW-TO

Take a moment when your child is already playing near you. Pause.

Take a long breath in, and let it all the way out.

Ask yourself: "What did I love to play when I was this age?"

Maybe you loved creating elaborate stories with toy animals, doing cartwheels, or drawing horses.

Take a moment to remember those feelings and sensations.

Remember what it felt like to be completely absorbed, when nothing else mattered except what you were doing.

Now look at your child. Could you join them, not as a parent supervising play, but as a fellow player? If you can, let yourself get absorbed in it the way you once did as a child.

As you join your child, pay attention to the sensations, like the sound of blocks clicking together or the smell of the crayons.

If (OK, when) you notice your mind wandering to chores or responsibilities, gently bring it back with another long breath in and out.

That's Hilarious

When was the last time you laughed so hard you just couldn't stop? When your stomach hurt and tears came into your eyes? The "church giggles," my grandmother used to call it. We mamas spend so much time holding everything together, managing everyone's needs, that we sometimes forget we're allowed to lose ourselves in ridiculous laughter—to whatever WE find funny. Our joy matters.

Plus, when your child sees you laughing your head off, they learn that adulthood contains joy, silliness, and moments of complete abandon. Your laughter is a gift to them too!

HOW-TO

Close your eyes and ask yourself: "When was the last time I laughed really, really hard?" As in possibly embarrassing, snort-inducing laughter.

Maybe it was that time when your toddler asked a wildly inappropriate question at your in-laws' house, or an inside joke you and your pals had in college.

As a memory comes into focus, allow yourself to relive it. Notice what happens in your body, just remembering. Maybe there's a genuine smile, maybe your shoulders drop down and relax.

Give yourself permission to think of something that YOU find funny, even if others might not get it.

Take another long breath in, and let it all the way out.

As you resume your day, consider how you could invite more of this kind of laughter into your life.

Maybe it's texting that friend with your same sense of humor, listening to a comedian you find hilarious while folding laundry, or reading that author you like who totally gets the absurdity of parenthood. Make it happen when you can.

Dance Like Nobody's Watching

I bet it's been a while since you moved your body just for fun. Not to get your steps in or to squeeze in that workout you "should" do, but just because it feels good. In the midst of the mental load that comes with being a parent, dancing with no agenda at all works like magic—it liberates you temporarily from the weight of responsibility and drops you into the pure joy of the moment. Your child inherently understands this as they twirl and shimmy without one bit of self-consciousness.

Dancing is also transformative in our brains: stress hormones like cortisol drop, while mood-boosting endorphins flood the system. It's powerful medicine for an overworked mind. If your child happens to be around, awesome—they can join in, or simply absorb the profound lesson that you're making time to move your body just for the joy of it.

HOW-TO

Put on a favorite song, something you really love (maybe something you forgot you love) with a great beat that makes you want to move.

Drop into your body. How does it want to move? Go for it.

Don't look in a mirror or try to catch your reflection in a window.

Think of how your child lets their body express joy. They twist, jump, and wiggle without worrying how they look.

Make sure you're breathing.

Bring awareness to your body as you dance. Where do you feel tense? Where are you holding back? Can you soften and move those places?

Start small and then let the movement grow, following what feels good. Remember how it felt to spin until you got dizzy? To wiggle your arms like cooked spaghetti? Try anything you like.

If you notice thoughts like "This is silly" or "I'm not a good dancer," just let them go with a long breath in and out.

This isn't for anyone else; it's for you. It's not a performance; you're not on a reality show.

Feel your heart beating and your breath quickening, telling you that your body is awake and alive in this moment.

Keep taking long breaths in and out.

Notice your mood. Observe if it's shifted at all.

Dance as long as it feels good!

Connection Activities

Watch me demonstrate all of these Let's Play activities, songs, and rhythm games, plus get the playlist, right here!

Free play is sacred territory for children—a world of their own making where the possibilities are endless. These mindful activities aren't meant to direct this precious time, but to offer playful jumping-off points that children can explore in their own way—invitations to adventure rather than instructions to follow.

Each activity honors how children naturally experience the world—through movement, imagination, and joy—while subtly weaving in mindful awareness of their bodies and emotions. Introduce these simple ideas and then step back, allowing children to take them in whatever direction they like.

Ha Ha Hyena

Release bottled-up energy and boost everyone's mood with this playful laughing exercise where pretend giggles quickly turn into real laughter. Do it together if you can, as this kind of silly joy is contagious! Add your favorite jokes or silly faces to keep the laughter going.

 **SONG PAIRING:** "Laugh a Little More"

SCRIPT

Imagine you're a hyena in the jungle.
Hyenas love to laugh!
Put your hands on your belly.
Take a breath in.
Start with a baby laugh: "Ha ha ha."
Take a breath in.
Laugh a little more: "Ha ha ha ha ha!"
Take a looong breath in.
"HA HA HA HA HA HA!"

Take a really looong breath in!
"HA HA HA HA HA HA!"
What's so funny, hyena?

IN THE CLASSROOM: Use this exercise as a quick energy-releasing activity during transitions. Students can sit, stand beside their desks, or gather in a circle; you could designate one student as the Head Hyena who gets to start each round of laughter. Finish with a "Freeze!" to come to stillness, and then a few long, slow breaths all together to get the last of the giggles out.

Rhythm & Rhyme Time

This flap-your-wings bumblebee rhyme lets kids be silly, buzzy bees; you'll know they're also calming their bodies with the long inhales followed by their best buzzing sounds. Watch it in action—use the QR code on page 122.

Fuzzy Buzzy Bumblebee

(*Make bumblebee wings by sticking elbows out to the sides. Flap them up and down and all around.*)

I'm a fuzzy buzzy bumblebee
My wings go up and down.
I'm a fuzzy buzzy bumblebee
I make a silly sound.
I go . . . (*Long breath in.*)
Bzzzzz!
I go . . . (*Long breath in.*)
Bzzzzz!
I'm a fuzzy buzzy bumblebee
You better watch out.
'Cause if you bother me
I might sting you!
OUCH!

Let's Go Swimming

Not getting to the beach anytime soon? No problem. Help children burn off excess energy through the full-body movement of "swimming" and then imagining the calming sensation of "floating." It's a nice balance of energetic play and relaxing body awareness. Play the song to really get the vibe going! And let your child expand on this however they like—maybe they go surfing, search for crabs, or have a beach picnic . . .

SONG PAIRING: "Make a Splash"

SCRIPT

Let's go swimming!
Ready? Jump into the water.
Lie down on your belly, and start swimming.
Can you use your arms as paddles?
Can you kick your feet?
Paddle! Kick! Paddle! Kick!
Can you swim faster?
Can you kick your feet?
Paddle! Kick! Paddle! Kick!
Even faster?
Whew! Time to rest.
Lie on your back.
Take a long breath in, and let it all the way out.
Float on the water.
Feel the sun on your face.
Relax your whole body.
Take another long breath in, and let it all the way out.
Just float.
Aaaahhh. . . .

IN THE CLASSROOM: Make a "swimming pool" in the classroom by pushing desks to the edges of the room or using the carpet area. Students can sit, stand, or lie on their bellies for the active "Paddle! Kick!" part of the exercise, and then move to a relaxing position or lie on their backs to "float." Make it extra fun and engaging by playing the song "Make a Splash"—and if time allows, let children "float" on their backs and relax for a few minutes in the quiet after the song ends.

Rhythm & Rhyme Time

This full-body wiggle fest takes kids from silly shimmying to peaceful breathing. Say it to a steady beat, then wind it down with long breaths in and out, hands on heart. (Use the QR code on page 122 to watch the video.)

The Shimmy

Shimmy shimmy high! (*Shake your hands up high.*)
Shimmy shimmy low! (*Shake your hands down low.*)
Shimmy shimmy in the pot nine days old. (*Make stirring-the-pot motions.*)
(*Repeat section.*)

Lift your shoulders up (*Lift shoulders toward ears.*)
Drop your shoulders down (*Let shoulders relax down.*)
Take your shoulders in your car all around the town. (*Grab your "steering wheel" and drive, make vroom-vroom sounds.*)
(*Repeat section.*)

Clap your hands together (*Clap once.*)
Rub 'em really fast (*Rub hands together.*)
Make some energy, make some energy
and breathe (*Long breath in and out, hands on heart.*)
and breathe. (*Long breath in and out, hands on heart.*)

Hush, Baby

Many children love to pretend they're caregivers, and this gentle rocking exercise soothes both the imaginary baby and the child themselves. Rhythmic side-to-side movements calm your child's busy body, and extended "Shh" sounds naturally slow their breathing. A lovely way to ease out of high-energy playtime.

SONG PAIRING: "Sleepy Eyes"

SCRIPT

Pretend you're rocking a baby to sleep.
Can you rock your baby in your arms?
Rock your baby.
Side to side, side to side.
Take a long breath in, and whisper "Shhhh . . ."
Rock your baby.
Side to side, side to side.
Take another long breath in.
Whisper "Shhhh . . ."
Make the "Shh" sound last as long as you can.
Is it working?
Try once more.
Rock your baby.
Side to side, side to side.
Take a long breath in, and whisper "Shhhh . . ."
Softly!
Baby's sleeping!

IN THE CLASSROOM: Let each student choose a small stuffed animal or soft classroom object to rock as they follow the exercise's calming side-to-side movements and breathing. It's a perfect transition activity for after lunch or recess or before focused work, when it's settle-down time.

Clouds

This dreamy activity encourages children to use their imagination to explore different emotional states while "floating" through the sky. Doing it outside while actually cloud-gazing is magical, but it works beautifully anywhere—even curled up on the couch on a rainy day.

**SONG PAIRING:** "How to Be a Cloud"

SCRIPT

Imagine you're a cloud in the sky.
You can be any kind of cloud you want.
What kind of a cloud are you?
Are you a white fluffy cloud, like a marshmallow?
Are you a dark gray storm cloud?
If you are, you can imagine your heavy raindrops falling down and far away.
Maybe you're a silly cloud, making shapes of jelly beans and polar bears.
Or maybe you're a sparkly cloud, full of snowflakes!
You can be any kind of cloud you want.
Take a long breath in, and let it all the way out.

IN THE CLASSROOM: Have students lie on the carpet or rest their heads on their desks, then guide them through the visualization as written, instructing them to answer the questions silently in their minds. Let them rest here as long as you can. Afterward, students can draw or write about what kind of cloud they were, or you can invite them to share aloud.

Rhythm & Rhyme Time

This empowering chant helps children build self-confidence and body awareness by spelling out "AWESOME" to a steady beat. This is a fun video to watch! (Use the QR code on page 122.)

A-W-E-S-O-M-E Chant

A-W-E-S-O-M-E! (*Say each letter in turn to a steady beat.*)
I am awesome
From my head to my feet.

A-W-E-S-O-M-E! (*Say each letter in turn to a steady beat.*)
I am awesome
And I love ME!

Create Something New

During mostly structured days, children rarely get the opportunity to stretch their imagination to its fullest. This exercise encourages creative thinking and mindful visualization, giving a kickstart to your child's creativity during playtime. Once they conjure up their invention in their mind, ask them to tell you all about it; you could invite them to draw or even make a prototype of it, making it as detailed as they like.

♫ **SONG PAIRING:** "Dream It Up"

SCRIPT

Let's invent something brand-new in our minds.
Inventing means to create something no one's even thought of yet!
What will you invent?
It can be anything you want.
Hmmm . . .
See your invention in your mind.
How big is it?
What color is it?

What does it do?
How does it work?
Your imagination is so powerful!
You can create anything you want in your mind.

IN THE CLASSROOM: Put students in pairs or small groups, and after the visualization, have students take turns describing, drawing, or writing about their invention. This can easily become a STEAM activity by having students present their inventions to the class or work in small groups to build prototypes. Create an "Invention Station" where students can post drawings or descriptions.

Together Time: Partner Connection Activity

Roller Coaster

This exercise is a delightful way for your child to release pent-up energy through big, joyful movement and have a blast with you at the same time. The roller-coaster theme taps into kids' natural love of pretend play. Magical when you add the song!

SONG PAIRING: "Roller Coaster"

HOW-TO

Sit on the floor with your legs crisscrossed or stretched out in a V shape. Have your child sit in front of you with their back to you, snuggled up close to your body or on your lap.

Hold your child's hands so you can do the arm motions together.

SCRIPT

Ready for a roller-coaster ride?
Let's hop into our roller-coaster car.
Take a deep breath in, and let it out. Here we go!

Let's twist our bodies side to side. Twist, twist, twist.

Now we're going up! Let's reach both arms up high. Up, up, up! (*Lean back for dramatic effect.*)

Wave your arms from side to side. Wheeee!

We're going back down. Down, down, down. (*Bring your arms down and lean forward.*)

We're turning a corner! (*Lean to one side.*)

Now we're turning the other way! (*Lean to the other side.*)

Here we go up again! Let's reach our arms up. Up, up, up! (*Lean back.*)

Wave them from side to side. Wheeee!

Now we're going back down. Down, down, down. (*Bring your arms down and lean forward.*)

Whew! Let's take a big breath in, and let it out.

That was fun!

(*Do it as many times as you like, then relax for a moment—maybe even lie all the way down and take a rest.*)

Let's Play-List

"Laugh a Little More"

Playful lyrics and a bouncy beat encourage children to embrace silliness and find humor in everyday moments.

"Make a Splash"

High-energy with Motown vibes, this rhythm-driven song invites children to jump, paddle, and kick as they "swim."

"Sleepy Eyes"

A soothing melody for rocking imaginary (or real) babies to sleep, lush and tranquil.

"How to Be a Cloud"

This gentle piano-based song relaxes children as they imagine they're clouds drifting peacefully through the sky.

"Dream It Up"

A whimsical, ukulele-based lullaby that invites children to visualize magical places and wonderful adventures (featuring kids' music superstar Laurie Berkner).

"Roller Coaster"

A musical roller-coaster ride complete with high-energy ups, downs, twists, and turns.

Your Turn

Create Space for Wonder and Play

Remember when you were a kid and spent hours absorbed in building with blocks or making up stories with your stuffed animals? That wasn't *just* play—that was essential brain development. Those stretches of unstructured time were laying the foundation for creativity, problem-solving, and emotional intelligence.

Your child needs those same kinds of experiences—they're just as crucial for their developing brain, if not more so, in our overstimulated world—but our hurry-up culture tries to rush children out of childhood, making this vital playtime increasingly rare.

Every time you resist the urge to schedule something during their free time or turn to a screen when they say they're bored, you're honoring your child's natural development and protecting what their brain desperately needs in order to grow. And here's what you can now create: space for your child's imagination to flourish, for them to get messy and make valuable mistakes, to figure things out on their own. Opportunities for true creativity that can't be taught in any class or on any app.

The tips and activities in this chapter are about joining your child's natural play in ways that deepen your connection, but they're more than that: they're helping you teach your child that curiosity and wonder are valuable, that joy matters, that being present is more important than being productive.

Your child doesn't need more "enrichment." They simply need the freedom to be exactly who they are right now—curious, imaginative, endlessly creative—and you have everything you need to give them that gift.

When you use these Calm & Connect steps, you'll Create:

More of This

- Curiosity and wonder
- Your child leading their own play
- Unhurried moments for your child to explore freely
- Open-ended play that sparks creativity and problem-solving
- Laughter and silliness that bubble up naturally
- Reconnecting with your own sense of play

Less of That

- Hustling from one activity to the next
- Feeling like a camp director in charge of entertainment
- Defaulting to screens when boredom strikes
- Worrying about the mess or chaos of free play
- Pressure to make every moment "educational"
- Forgetting how to have fun

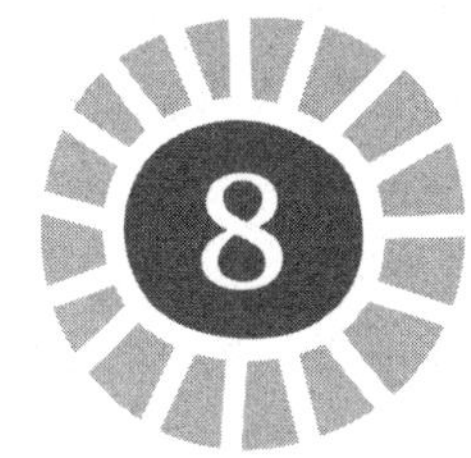

Time to Eat

Ending the Mealtime Madness and Creating Connection Around the Table

IT SOUNDS SILLY, but this truth hit me like a ton of bricks when my three children were little: these tiny human people needed to eat THREE WHOLE MEALS every single day. I really felt like someone should have taken me aside and warned me. Every day when I had just about finished cleaning up breakfast, it was lunchtime; snacks were required every twenty minutes throughout the afternoon; and all day, every day, dinner prep was breathing down my neck.

Having children means you're signing up for approximately 1,095 meals together per year, not counting snacks (so many snacks). That's roughly 19,710 chances before they leave the nest to either pull your hair out or approach those meals as opportunities to strengthen your relationship and bring some joy and a feeling of togetherness to the table. And yet, most of us are just trying to get through the meal without tears—while secretly hoping for just two minutes where everyone actually talks to each other instead of complaining about what's on their plate.

Why It's Hard

Ah, family dinner: where your expectations go to die. Hunger and fatigue are ramping up, and it perfectly coincides with the "witching hour," when everyone's emotional regulation skills have left the building.

Our parents' generation plunked us down to eat in front of the TV with microwaved lasagna and zero guilt. But then we became parents and we had visions of screen-free, mindful family dinners where everyone shares thoughtful reflections while eagerly trying new foods. Instead, it's like hosting a tiny, ungrateful focus group each night.

There's the impossible math of feeding multiple children with different preferences—one wants pasta with no sauce, another will eat only sauce with no pasta, and the third has decided she's gluten-free today. You're left feeling like an unappreciated server at a twenty-four-hour diner. Maybe there's guilt about the quick and easy dinner you threw together or picked up because work ran late. Or you spend an hour and a half making a nutritious, well-rounded dinner, and your child eats exactly one bite. Meanwhile, social media gleefully shows you moms who meal prep for a month at a time and make peanut butter cups from scratch.

Of course, then we're left with cleaning up the kitchen, which is now an absolute crime scene. (When it was dish-doing time, my boys often desperately had to go to the bathroom and then never reappeared, or suddenly remembered a homework assignment that needed starting ASAP. Happens to this day.) And all of this is happening during the time of day when your own tank is nearly empty.

Mealtime with young children can feel like a hot mess (quite literally), but it doesn't have to be this way.

What If . . .

Instead of the inevitable nightly meltdown zone, what if dinnertime was—dare I say it—something you actually looked forward to? Picture a few minutes of relative calm at the table, moments of genuine connection with your child from meeting them in their world. I won't paint this with too rosy a brush; of all the challenging daily transitions we navigate with children, this one is toward the top of the list. But mealtime goes a whole lot more smoothly when you work with your children's natural wiring instead of battling against their need for movement, their difficulty transitioning, or their sensitivities.

I hate to say it, but these years when children actually want to sit at the table with you are fleeting. Blink and they'll be teenagers with mysterious social lives, and you'll be lucky when they grace you with their presence. The foundation you build now—using a child-centered, mindful approach that honors how your child actually operates—can create the kind of moments you'll all actually remember in years to come.

The tips and strategies in this chapter are about creating space for more joy, more participation, and even a little more calm by weaving mindful presence into the playful, physical, imaginative ways children already experience the world. The goal isn't perfect behavior or perfect dinners (not in my house, at least). The goal is meaningful togetherness and connection, built one meal at a time.

Setting the Stage: Tips for Calmer Mealtimes

Have a clear vision. Having clarity around what actually matters to you (and your partner or co-parent, if you have one) can be a game changer. Ask yourself: What is truly important to you at mealtime? Is it five minutes of everyone sitting at the table together? Set a timer. Is it that your child learns to eat in one spot instead of while wandering? Make that your priority. Maybe it's that they chew with their mouth closed, or that they can take a lap around the house when they need to move, but then they have to come back to their seat. Whatever it is, name it so everyone is clear.

Create distinct bookends to your meals, so snacks and dinners have defined beginnings and endings. You could start with a "shake it out" break to burn excess energy, then a simple deep breath all together before eating. End with a consistent signal that mealtime is complete—does your child need to ask to be excused? Is dinner not over until you say it is? You decide, and establish expectations.

Keep the bar relatively low, and developmentally appropriate. Your three-year-old probably isn't going to sit quietly for twenty minutes, and that's as it should be. Worry less about the social decorum and more about the connection created. Later in this chapter I'll give you ideas for specific, quick, child-friendly strategies to try; even the tiniest mindful practice can transform the energy at your table.

Looking back, I'd tell my younger self to lighten up at mealtime and to stop worrying that my children as grown-ups would still be sitting under the table eating with their hands. I wish I'd known then to cast a more realistic vision focused on togetherness, not perfection. I'd have prioritized making it more fun to be at the table together while they were little, even with the mess. (It will be messy no matter what.)

Create a vision that works for your family, in your real life. Those small moments of connection—even amid the chaos—are what they'll remember.

Include your child in the prep. Involving children in meal planning and preparation turns mealtime into an opportunity for shared responsibility, learning, and togetherness, not to mention culinary adventure. Even very young children can set the table, stir the soup in the pot, or push the buttons on the microwave. When kids help plan, shop, and cook—even in very small ways—they develop a sense of ownership over the meal that makes them more likely to sit down and actually eat what's served. It can change "What IS this?" into "Try my soup!" pretty fast.

The time spent cooking together creates natural opportunities for conversation, too. Stirring a pot side by side encourages an easy dialogue that might feel easier than the "How was school?" questions at the table. That twenty minutes of (flour-covered, giggly) "cooking" might just be your best intelligence-gathering operation of the day.

Plus, involving your child in prep creates a natural bridge between playtime and dinnertime, providing a wind-down period where your child can shift their energy and attention rather than being abruptly called to the table from play, which can feel jarring and unwelcome. Now sitting down at the table feels like a natural progression. Yay! We made it (or heated it up, or had it delivered, whatever) together; now it's time to eat it. Let's sit!

Beyond just getting your child to the table more easily, your kitchen adventures are secretly building your child's arsenal of life skills. As they measure ingredients, they're absorbing math concepts, learning how to follow recipes, and learning cooking techniques they'll need down the road. You're saving them from living on ramen later! Look at you go.

Now let's be real. Having your five-year-old help measure flour will absolutely take twice as long and create a small snowstorm in your kitchen. There will be spills, drips, and eggshells to fish out. Stirring becomes an aerobic activity. (I think I've said "Remember we need to keep the sauce IN the pan" about a million times.) If you're a type-A personality, you'll have heart palpitations as your child mixes batter like a tiny tornado. Deep breaths, Mama. It's totally worth it.

When children see meal prep as a shared family responsibility rather than something that magically happens, they're connecting the dots between grocery store, garden, and plate, and are more likely to develop a healthy relationship with food. They're seeing food as something created with effort and care, not something that just mysteriously appears every time they're hungry. Which is basically all the time.

Don't give too many choices. Lots of options are overwhelming for young children. Their developing brains aren't equipped to handle decision overload, especially when they're already tired and hungry. Asking them an open-ended "What do you want for dinner?" turns mealtime into one long back-and-forth negotiation, and you are not a short-order cook. Keeping choices to a minimum isn't about restriction—it's about creating the calm, clear boundaries that allow connection to be the priority at the table.

Consistency beats variety most days. I love this quote about meal prep from the wonderful book *Simplicity Parenting* by Kim John Payne (10/10 recommend): "You are not staging a new Broadway production, from concept to performance, every night." Amen. A predictable rhythm of meals—even if it sometimes feels boring—provides the structure and predictability that young children crave.

You can still give them choices—just be sure either option works for you: "Would you like the yellow spoon or the blue spoon?" or "Carrots or an apple with your sandwich?" Don't concede your authority. You're in charge, and your child needs you to be—they actually feel more secure when parents confidently make the big decisions.

Always include a "Yes, please" food—something you know they'll eat. This creates safety and security while encouraging them to try unfamiliar foods alongside something familiar. We're not going for perfect nutrition at every meal; we're building a positive relationship with food over time.

Quick story: to say my son was a picky eater is an understatement; he had an extraordinarily limited diet as a young child. Before we understood that he had sensory challenges and acute sensitivities (he was eventually diagnosed as a "super taster"), what I'm really proud of was that mealtime never became a power struggle. I always made sure there was something he would eat, and we kept the discussion about it at the table to a minimum. Even at Thanksgiving, when the table was loaded with dozens of food choices, I simply pulled out the package of pretzels I had brought for him, and that was that.

Finally, and I know you know this, but I'll say it anyway: keep it relatively healthy, with foods that you mostly recognize from nature. There are some truly alarming, created-in-a-lab synthetic things marketed as "kid food" these days. The crinkly packages! The bright colors! They're so fun to look at, but let's do our best to steer clear.

Create easy "special occasions." The simplest change of scenery can transform the whole vibe at mealtime. Indoor picnics are where it's at—something about being on the floor makes everything more appealing to kids. It's basically their natural habitat anyway. Spread a blanket on the living room floor and lay out the food picnic-style; suddenly the same chicken they'd ignore at the table becomes fascinating fare worth trying.

Other ideas: turn off the lights and have a candlelit dinner once a week—we called it "fancy dinner." Battery-operated tea lights work just fine. Your child will consider it fine dining, and you haven't done anything more complicated than flick a few switches. You could head into another room and eat around the coffee table. Move it outside if the weather is nice. Let everyone sit under the table! The location doesn't matter; the novelty does.

The beauty is that these ideas require almost zero additional energy, which is exactly what we're going for. You're prepping the food no matter what; you're just changing where and how it's served. These small, easy shifts can make the difference between a meal that drains you further when you're already running on empty and one that actually creates joy and connection by feeling special and different to both you and your child.

Trust your gut, not the peanut gallery. When my son was refusing most foods, the uninvited opinions poured in: "Oh, he'll eat it when he's hungry enough." (Nope.) "He'll eat the snack at school when he sees the other kids eating it." (Also no.) The well-meaning chorus of voices implied that everything would magically resolve if I just followed their advice. Meanwhile, my actual child went right on eating his same few foods, completely unbothered by their theories.

Others don't see the full context, and it's not your job to explain it to anyone outside of your immediate family. Whether it's paper plates for dinner, iPads in the restaurant, or mac and cheese for the third time this week, let the guilt go—you're doing what works for your family, and that's what matters.

Try not to compare, or to judge. That mom letting her child use her phone and headphones at a restaurant? Her child might have auditory processing issues that make the environment overwhelming otherwise. The parents serving a different meal to each child could be navigating sensory challenges or medical needs. We just don't know what's actually happening inside someone else's family.

I watched *M*A*S*H* on TV with my grandmother every single night while we ate, and look how well I turned out. (It was on twice each night; she'd ask me after school: "Shall we have our supper at five thirty or at seven?") It was what worked for us. To be clear, I don't recommend this, but the point is that there's no one right way to do it.

The measure of mealtime success isn't how fancy your table looks or whether you're following someone else's formula. It's whether your approach supports your family's unique needs, creates space for connection, and keeps everyone reasonably nourished without driving you bonkers.

One of my better parenting moves was trusting my gut on my son's eating patterns. By honoring his process rather than forcing the matter, I built a trust with him that has truly lasted. Prioritizing our relationship over the "rules" created space for him to develop healthy eating patterns on his own timeline.

Listen to your child, not the crowd. Let others think and say what they will—you can't control them anyway, so you might as well save your breath. Tune in to your child's actual needs. Do what genuinely works for the beautiful, complex, real-life family that's right in front of you. Real connection happens in this relaxed and authentic space.

Mama Mantra

Relationship over rules.

Let go of the outcome. I went through a phase of preparing healthy after-school snacks for my young children. I'd set a proper table with sliced fruit and veggies, wholesome crackers and cheese. The phase was quite short, because my children walked right past it (my son actually asked, "Who's that for?") and headed straight to the cupboard to forage for something sweet.

Truth time: We can prepare and serve the most fabulous, nutritious food, but we cannot make our children eat it. We can set the table using the fun plates and the favorite cups, but we can't script how mealtime unfolds. The sooner we release our tight grip on these outcomes, the more peace and joy we'll find at the table. (The mindfulness exercise we'll explore later in this chapter—My Job Is Done—is perfect for practicing this letting go.)

I get it. You've chopped, prepped, and plated, carefully considered various preferences, and maybe even arranged the carrot sticks into a smiley face. You want them to EAT IT.

But read any of the books on getting your child to eat—I've read most of them—and you'll likely find a version of this advice from the nutrition experts and feeding specialists: your job ends at providing good food in a reasonably pleasant environment. Period. Your child's job is deciding what and how much to eat from what you've offered. This is super important: when we blur these boundaries, meals become power struggles.

You're playing the long game here. Your consistent, no-pressure offering of varied foods, your willingness to let go of control, and your modeling of healthy eating lay the foundation for your child to develop their own healthy relationship with food.

So, once you've done your job, take a breath and release the outcome—you've done what you can do.

It takes a village. In other words, ask for help. Being the only person responsible for getting food on the table every night is a surefire recipe (ahem) for resentment. No dinnertime heroics, please. You're already drained from a long day.

The mostly invisible mental load of planning, shopping, preparing, and serving meals day after day requires enormous time, energy, and emotional bandwidth—yet often goes completely unacknowledged.

Pull back the curtain. Talk openly about how much you do and how you could divide the load. Will your partner make different meals than you would? Probably. (Pro tip: resist the strong urge to micromanage.) Will the timing be off? Almost certainly. Is it worth it? A million percent yes. Distributing the work isn't just giving you a break—it's creating room for you to be the mindful, present parent you want to be at the table.

Consider expanding your mealtime village. Sharing meals with other families works a special kind of magic—it takes some of the pressure off you as the sole meal provider and creates a novel environment where children witness different types of dishes, eating habits, and family dynamics in action. (Don't underestimate the power of your child watching their pal eat the broccoli either.)

The back-and-forth of welcoming each other to your tables establishes a comforting pattern where everyone contributes and everyone benefits. When I shared regular meals with a close mom friend whose children were similar ages to mine, the fun far outweighed the chaos. We were outnumbered five to two in a whirlwind of small people and endless requests, but we were in it together, finding humor and solidarity. The children loved this break from routine; it felt like a celebration. What stands out in my memory isn't the logistics or mess, but how much we laughed.

Mama Mantra

Connection beats control.

Particularly if you're solo parenting, building a network of dinner allies—whether it's trading childcare so you each get time to meal prep, hosting a weekly potluck, or having a standing dinner date with another family—can make the endless cycle of meals feel less isolating and give you room to breathe, literally and figuratively.

So ask yourself honestly: Are you being a martyr about dinner? Stop that, please. When you're not trying to do it all alone, you have the capacity to be fully present and create joyful moments of togetherness with your child. And those are what truly matters.

Calm Starts with You

This is a tough time to ask you to be mindful, I know. Everyone's hungry, including you, and the wheels are coming right off the wagon. These quick exercises focus on creating small moments to ground yourself in the midst of family life. No one's asking you to be a zen master while cooking and managing mealtime, but sometimes a single conscious breath is all we need to shift our energy and keep going. Here are some practical strategies to try.

Mama Mantra
The table is for togetherness.

What's in the Cupboard

You know that moment when you open your kitchen cupboard at 5:30 PM, staring at the shelves like they'll tell you the answer to what's for dinner? And then you start thinking: you really need to meal plan like all those momfluencers do, it can't be that hard, and you decide you'll definitely start this Sunday, but then you remember your kids actually have that thing Sunday, so you'll start the following weekend . . . Hold it right there. Instead of letting overwhelm take over, let's turn this into your secret reset button. This simple mindfulness exercise is private, quick, and truly helpful.

HOW-TO

Open your cupboard door (or wherever you survey your available ingredients).

Pause, bringing your attention to your feet on the floor.

Take a long breath in, and let it all the way out.

Slowly move your eyes over the shelves.

Notice the options in front of you.

Take a long breath in, and let it all the way out.

Let your shoulders drop and your jaw relax.

Notice the shapes, sizes, and colors of the items you see.

One more long breath in, and let it all the way out.

Silently remind yourself: "I am feeding my family. It's enough."

The First Bite

Eating an entire meal mindfully while managing the chaos of dinnertime is probably not going to happen (OK, there's really no chance). But we can claim just one bite as a tiny moment of presence and peace. This quick exercise grounds you in the current moment and helps you actually taste, and hopefully enjoy, your food. More than that, it creates a tiny ritual of self-care during hectic family meals and models mindful eating for your child. If they ask what the heck you're doing, tell them and maybe they'll join you!

HOW-TO

Take one long breath in and out, feeling your body in the chair.

Look at your first bite of food, noticing its colors, textures, and how it's arranged on your fork or spoon.

As you lift the food to your mouth, pause briefly to smell your bite.

Place the food in your mouth, but don't chew yet.

Close your eyes if you want to, for just a moment. (This is definitely when your child's curiosity will kick in.)

Begin to chew slowly, noticing the initial flavor, the temperature of the food, and the textures as they change.

Pay attention to the food traveling down your throat as you swallow it.

Open your eyes and carry on. Try for another mindful bite if you can!

My Job Is Done

Much as we'd like to, we can't do a single thing to control our children's tastes or their choices. You cannot make the food appeal to them, and you cannot eat for them. That's not your job. Your job was to offer good food, and you've done that. Try this to help release a bit of that tight grip on the outcome. Every meal or snack is a new opportunity to practice this.

HOW-TO

At the start of the meal, maybe as you set the last dish down on the table, take a moment to really look at what's in front of you.

Pause. Notice the colors of the food, the steam rising from a hot dish, the familiar shapes of plates and cups.

Take a long breath in and out, and silently say: "My job is done."

Take another long breath in. With your exhale, release your hold on the outcome: the worry about whether your child will like it, the frustration with their complaining, the urge to cajole or negotiate.

Anytime you feel frustrated during the meal, return to your breath and these words: "My job is done."

As best you can, practice being present at the table with your family.

Connection Activities

Watch me demonstrate all of these Time to Eat activities, songs, and rhythm games, plus get the playlist, right here!

These work with your child's natural curiosity and playfulness. By focusing on presence instead of "perfect" behavior, these simple practices transform eating from another daily task into opportunities for genuine connection. Plus, they plant seeds for healthier relationships with food, while making meals a lot more fun. Here are some bite-sized mindfulness moments to bring to your family table.

Slow Like a Sloth

Do you have a gobble monster who's done with their food by the time you sit down? Let's see what we can do about that. By imagining they're nature's slowest and most deliberate eater, children can practice eating mindfully while being dramatic and having a ball.

SONG PAIRING: "Peaceful Like a Panda"

SCRIPT

Let's eat like sloths!
A sloth is an animal that moves really, really slowly.
Pick up your fork slowly.
You're in slow motion!
How slowly can you move?
Bring your food to your mouth, even more slowly.
How slowly can you chew?
I'll count to twenty. (*Have your child chew while you slowly count to twenty out loud.*)
Whew! Let's take a break.
In slow motion, put your fork down.

Breathe in, breathe out.
Breathe in, breathe out.
(*Continue as long as you like.*)

IN THE CLASSROOM: Read the script as written during your students' first bite or two of lunch or snack, cultivating present-moment attention and helping children practice impulse control. It's also a perfect addition to an animal-themed lesson plan.

Food Explorers

The focus here is on the exciting "discovery" of a new food, rather than the reaction to it (you just have to let that go). A successful expedition is about being brave enough to try!

SONG PAIRING: "Super Senses"

SCRIPT

Let's be Food Explorers!
We're going to discover a new food today.
Look at your plate with your telescope. (*Make circles around your eyes with your hands.*)
What do you see? (*Invite your child to answer these questions aloud.*)
Is your food orange or red, white or green? Or another color?
Now take an explorer sniff.
What do you smell?
Does it smell spicy or sweet?
Or like something else?
Now for the bravest part of our expedition.
Take a small bite of your discovery.
What does it taste like?
Is it warm or cold?
How would you talk about it to another explorer?
Well done, explorer!

IN THE CLASSROOM: Transform snack time into an "Explorer's Expedition" where your class tries one new food all together using this script. Have students share, draw, or journal their observations, noting colors, textures, and flavors. Make it into more of a lesson by mapping where foods originate, talking about nutritional values, or challenging students to "eat the rainbow" by tracking color diversity in the foods they eat.

Rhythm & Rhyme Time

Try this simple gratitude rhyme with your child as a quick mindful moment before eating. The rhythmic clapping after each line helps focus wandering attention. You can watch the video, too—use the QR code on page 145.

Thank You Song

Thanks for our table (*Clap clap.*)
Thanks for this food (*Clap clap.*)
Thanks for this time (*Clap clap.*)
For me and you! (*Clap clap, then long breath in and out.*)

Ask Your Belly

Through gentle breathing and body awareness, this playful exercise guides children to pause, check in with their body, and make mindful choices about eating—helping them develop a healthy relationship with food.

**SONG PAIRING:** "How Do I Feel?"

SCRIPT

Should you eat a few more bites? (*Invite your child to answer these questions aloud.*)

Or are you full?
Well, ask your belly!
Take a long breath in, and let it out.
Close your eyes if it helps.
Put one hand on your belly.
Say: "Belly, how do you feel?"
Pay attention. What does your belly say?
You might need to ask again.
Say: "Hey, belly, how do you feel?"
Pay attention. What does your belly say?
Do you feel full?
Or do you need to eat a little bit more?
Breathe in, and breathe out.
You know what to do!

IN THE CLASSROOM: Read the script as written to students toward the middle or end of eating time, and invite them to share their answers. "Asking" their belly helps children develop the critical skill of self-awareness and teaches them to tune in to their bodies. It paves the way for them to recognize other bodily cues related to emotions, helping them regulate themselves more easily in the classroom and elsewhere.

Kindness

This simple reflection exercise helps children recognize and celebrate acts of kindness—both given and received—helping them build empathy and awareness of how their actions affect others. Invite your child to share after each question. You could share your own answers too!

SONG PAIRING: "Thank You"

SCRIPT

Think of something kind that someone else did for you.
(*Pause between lines, giving your child plenty of time to think about each instruction.*)

How did it make you feel?
Think of something kind you've done for someone else.
Maybe you helped someone in your family at home, or you helped a friend at school.
How did it make you feel?
Now think of something kind that you haven't done yet, but you will, the next time you have the chance.
Is there someone you could help, or say some kind words to?
Try to remember to do that kind thing when you can.
Take a long breath in, and let it all the way out.

IN THE CLASSROOM: Use this exercise as part of a lesson on kindness, or make kindness a part of your classroom culture as a daily exercise. Invite children to share the acts of kindness they think of out loud or by drawing or writing them. Create a "Random Acts of Kindness" board where you track students' kind words or gestures. Consider incorporating kindness service projects, like making cards or drawings for nursing homes.

Thanks for the Food

This gentle gratitude practice encourages children to connect with their food's journey to your table, helping them recognize and appreciate the many hands that helped bring them their meal.

 **SONG PAIRING:** "Where's It From?"

SCRIPT

Take a long breath in, and let it all the way out.
Someone grew the food you're eating today.
Let's say thank you to the person who grew it.
Thank you!
Someone put your food in a package.
Let's say thank you to the person who put it in a package.
Thank you!
Someone served you that food.

Let's say thank you to the person who served it to you.
Thank you!
Take a long breath in, and let it all the way out.

IN THE CLASSROOM: Incorporate gratitude into your classroom by exploring the journey food takes to reach your students' lunch tables. Guide children to trace their food backward–from their trays to the cafeteria staff, delivery drivers, and the farmers who nurture crops and tend animals. Create a "Gratitude Map" showing these connections, and pause before or during eating to acknowledge these often invisible helpers. This practice can extend beyond food–you can make a lesson out of tracing the complex pathways behind everyday items like pencils, clothing, or classroom furniture.

Rhythm & Rhyme Time

A playful countdown rhyme that turns the transition to mealtime into a rhythmic game, giving children both structure and fun as they find their way to the table. (Use the QR code on page 145 to watch the video.)

Table Time

Table time, table time
Everybody find their seat.
Table time, table time
Let's march to the beat!

Ten, nine, eight . . . (*Count down as fast or as slow as you like, allowing your child to find their seat, then continue when seated.*)

Table time, table time
Everybody's in their seat.
Table time, table time
Now it's time to breathe. (*Take a slow breath in and out together.*)

The Mixing Bowl

This exercise is a sweet opportunity for you and your child to connect through gentle movement and stretching: the circular rocking motion is calming, and the partner stretches release tension in the body. A unique shared activity like this helps smooth the transition to mealtime or can bridge the gap afterward between dinner and bedtime. Make sure you play the song!

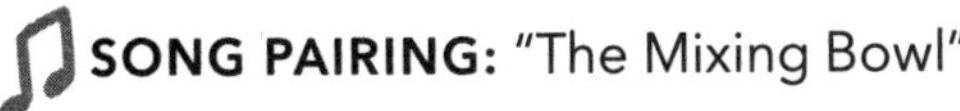

SONG PAIRING: "The Mixing Bowl"

HOW-TO

Sit on the floor facing your child. Your legs can be either in a wide V shape or crisscrossed.

Make all the motions of starting to bake something yummy: crack your imaginary eggs, open the flour, pour in some sugar, and whatever else you like. (If you're listening to the song, just follow along with the lyrics.)

Sit tall and hold each other's hands. Like you're stirring batter in a mixing bowl, slowly begin to move your upper bodies in a gentle circular motion, ideally to the rhythm of the song. Keep the movement smooth and steady.

Pause for a moment for a stretch. Keeping a steady grip on your child's hands, gently pull them toward you as you lean back, and hold for a breath or two.

Then switch. Let them gently pull you forward as they lean back, holding for a moment.

Then resume "stirring" in your mixing bowl for as long as you like.

Make it more of a fun game by deciding what kind of treat you're baking, and gobble it up when you're done!

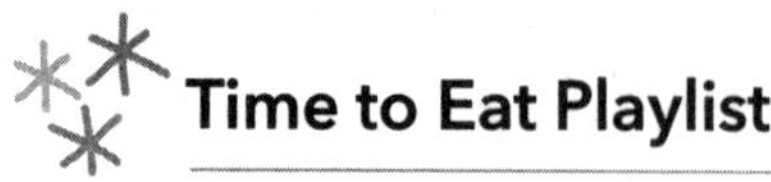

Time to Eat Playlist

"Peaceful Like a Panda"

Playful and light, celebrating a carefree panda bear who lives a slow, stress-free life full of simple pleasures.

"Super Senses"

Encourages children to discover the wonders of the world around them through their senses, with a stealthy bass line and a secret agent vibe.

"How Do I Feel?"

A gentle, sweet song that helps children tune in to physical and emotional signals from their bodies, giving them confidence to ask for what they need.

"Thank You"

A catchy and easy-to-sing message of gratitude for our families, friends, and people who care about us.

"Where's It From?"

Invites children to get curious about the origins of familiar objects and foods they eat every day.

"The Mixing Bowl"

Warm and mellow, this acoustic guitar-driven tune wraps you in the comfort of a cozy kitchen.

Create Mealtime Memories That Matter

Now you have the tools to create exactly the kind of mealtime culture you've always wanted for your family. Using the tips and activities in this chapter, you can establish rituals that bring genuine joy to your table and build new traditions your child will carry into adulthood.

Think about the shift: Instead of feeling like you're constantly negotiating with tiny food critics, you become the guide who helps them explore and enjoy eating. Instead of dinnertime being something you dread, it becomes a time when you genuinely connect with your child through curiosity, play, and presence.

Your child doesn't need you to be a personal chef or a dinner drill sergeant. They need you to meet them where they are, with their wiggly bodies and unpredictable appetites, and help them develop a healthy, joyful relationship with food that will last.

The kitchen will still get messy. But now you have the tools to transform that chaos into genuine family connection and create the mealtime memories you want your children to carry forward.

When you use these Calm & Connect steps, you'll Create:

More of This

Togetherness and engagement at the table

Being OK with imperfect, messy meals

Flexibility with food preferences and eating styles

Shared responsibility and pride when you involve your child as a helper

Moments of calm presence amid the dinner chaos

Lasting memories with easy "special occasions" and mealtime traditions

Less of That

Comparing to other families or moms on social media

Feeling like a short-order cook at a twenty-four-hour diner

Worrying about your child's future eating habits

Dreading dinnertime during the day

Battling over bites

Expecting good manners and thoughtful conversation from an over-tired child

Good Night

Winding Down (Even on Hard Days) with Closeness and Calm

I'M ARMY-CRAWLING across my daughter Lola's bedroom floor with the stealth of a ninja. One wrong move—a creaky floorboard, a tiny yelp when I encounter a Lego—and her batlike ears will detect my escape attempt. After waiting what feels like hours for her to finally drift off, I'm not taking any chances. I reach the doorway—victory is mine!—and a small voice pipes up: "Mommy? Where goin'?"

Back to square one.

If you've ever found yourself trapped in your child's room, afraid to breathe too loudly lest you restart the whole bedtime process, you're not alone. Getting children to go to sleep (and stay asleep), in my humble opinion, is one of parenting's greatest challenges. And it can feel terribly isolating when, at least according to Instagram, everyone else's children apparently conk out by 7:30 PM sharp (freshly bathed, with tomorrow's outfit neatly laid out).

Why It's Hard

The bedtime struggle is real for so many reasons. For starters, there's the endless resistance and stalling: "I'm not tired!" (despite barely being able to keep their eyes open) or "Wait, I forgot to tell you something!" (suddenly remembering many, many tiny but crucial details of their day).

Then there's anxiety, which can transform your independent-in-the-daytime child into a barnacle, and often peaks at bedtime when separation from you looms. This is when children unload all the worries and big emotions that have built up inside them all day. You want to give them your full attention, with all the empathy of the great mama that you are, but your own tank is running on empty and all you can think about is that lights-out is getting later and later.

For families juggling older kids' activities (9 PM indoor soccer games? whyyyy) or managing two households, maintaining consistent bedtime routines can feel nearly impossible. Add in sensory issues around the "right" pjs, having the blanket spread out just so, and the white noise volume that was perfect yesterday but is "too swooshy" tonight, and you've got an endless game of bedtime whack-a-mole that can stretch until midnight.

I'm pretty sure you know this already, but inadequate sleep in children is problematic in all kinds of ways. The short version: tired kids have a much harder time controlling themselves, paying attention, and managing their feelings. Fatigue not only causes increased irritability but also makes emotions run high, making everyday challenges way harder. If your child had any frustration tolerance to begin with, now it's at zero.

And strangely enough, being overtired often makes children more hyper, not less, and this combined with struggling to pay attention makes for a tough time at school as well as at home. (Exhausted children are also more likely to get sick. Not what we need.)

Beyond those not-so-lovely effects, what's closer to home, so to speak, is what a child not sleeping well does to the household. Here I'm a certified, card-carrying expert.

My oldest had a terrible time going to sleep as a young child. And I mean every single night. It was a disaster that unfolded at a glacial pace; we were in survival mode until she was nearly four. A pediatrician told me once: the less they sleep, the less they sleep—and for a long, long time she was living proof of just how true that is.

I didn't put on a nice outfit or think a coherent thought for about three years. I was always exhausted, falling asleep in the car in the preschool pickup line, feeling alone since it seemed like all my friends' kids slept just fine, forgetting what my husband looked like since we never ate dinner together. Just getting the basics done felt like running a daily marathon.

The house was always a mess, which made me feel angry pretty much all the time, and our daughter's sleep troubles were still very much happening when our next child was born, so you can imagine how not awesome it was, sleep-wise, to add an infant to the mix.

The lessons I eventually learned about helping children settle at bedtime came a little too late for my first two children. It wasn't until our third arrived that I finally had the tools in my toolbox to create a bedtime routine that worked for all of us, full of (mostly) peaceful moments together.

(And when I finally started getting it together to put on clothes that kind of made an outfit and weren't 100 percent stretchy, my daughter would eye me suspiciously and say, "Why are you fancy?")

What If . . .

What if bedtime could feel different? Imagine this for a moment: Instead of sensing that bedtime is about rushing them to lights-out, your child actually looks forward to it as special connection time with you. The nighttime routine flows predictably for everyone. There's been a fundamental shift; now it's way less "go-to-sleep-NOW" and more about closing the day together in a way that feels right for your family.

Picture yourself confident enough in your routine that occasional departures from it don't derail the whole thing. You've learned how to use kid-friendly movement and stretches, mindfulness, and the right music to help your child settle naturally into sleep. Most important, you've shifted your focus from compliance (not my favorite word, but accurate here) to connection, building trust with your child.

And here's something revolutionary—you actually have time for yourself afterward. You've set up a sustainable system that works for everyone, including you. Yes, you.

Bedtime gives us a precious opportunity to cultivate deep, mindful connections with our children that can far outlast childhood. By practicing presence and establishing routines that suit children's natural temperaments now, we create more than just a peaceful path to sleep—we build trust, emotional safety, and strong bonds.

I know firsthand how challenging sleep struggles can be; those neverending evenings of tears and resistance that leave everyone feeling depleted and discouraged. But as I've discovered, these child-friendly strategies not only ease current bedtime struggles; they also lay the foundation for lasting connection.

So whether you're hoping to enhance an already solid bedtime routine or you're in the trenches with sleep challenges, the hard-won strategies in this chapter might be exactly what you're looking for.

Here are some tips to try.

Setting the Stage: Tips for a Calmer Bedtime

Get yourself ready first. My friend Sarah does this, and I love it. I wish I had done this when my three were little! Take care of your own bedtime basics before starting your child's routine—change into your "cozies," grab your water, wash your face. When your child is asleep, you'll be all set to actually enjoy the peaceful house instead of dragging yourself through your own routine. (And for those nights when you fall asleep with your child and wake up groggy and confused, you'll be so grateful you already brushed your teeth.)

Taking care of your own needs and energy before your child's bedtime isn't selfish—it's actually essential for you to be able to create the intentional connection your child needs at this vulnerable time.

Related: make sure you're taking good care of yourself throughout the day. Carve out a few minutes for yourself when you can. Eat well, stay hydrated. You know what to do. Not only is this good for your overall well-being, but it helps prevent the desperate craving for alone time that leads to rushing through bedtime.

The honest situation is this: your child wants more of you in the evening, and you (probably) want less of them. It doesn't mean you don't love them to pieces, but by 7 PM you are likely toast and ready for the couch (or whatever feels relaxing to you). I get it. Just remember this is a big reason why this time of day is hard, and why taking care of yourself is so critically important.

Mama Mantra

Grace over guilt.

Get moving to get the sillies out. It might seem like the opposite of what you should do before bed, but active movement can actually help children calm down, because exertion triggers the body's natural relaxation response. Physical activity not only burns off excess energy, but releases feel-good endorphins and increases the production of sleep-promoting hormones. The key here is gradually decreasing the intensity, which signals that it's time to switch from active to rest mode. A few ideas:

- Have a mini dance party to a song that starts with high-energy and ends on a calm note (a great one is "All I Wanna Do Is Dance").
- Act out different animals, starting with roaring lions, stomping dinosaurs, or shaking puppies, moving to cozy koalas or baby birds getting ready for sleep.
- Play follow the leader: let your child lead first and do whatever they want, then you take your turn and move from hopping, jumping, and stomping to super-slooow-motion tiptoes, leading right into bed.

Power down. Screen time before bed significantly impacts children's sleep quality. I know this is a tough one, so I've come with stats: In a systematic review, researchers found that 90 percent of published studies conclude that screen time has a significant negative impact on children's sleep duration, timing, and quality. The National Sleep Foundation also reviewed a huge number of studies and scholarly articles on this topic, putting out a statement in August 2024 concluding that screen use impairs sleep health among children.

I'm so serious about this: please keep screens out of kids' bedrooms. There's just no upside here. Establish clear boundaries around device use early, since managing screen time becomes way harder as children grow older. Have a designated overnight spot for devices, like a kitchen drawer. For special shows, watch them before dinner when possible. Create a device-free wind-down routine before bed.

I can tell you this from experience: Future You will be so, so glad you helped children build healthy, sustainable habits around screens now. They'll carry them forward as they grow. When your child is a teenager and needs to surrender their device for the night, it will be a million times easier if it's been a clear household rule since childhood.

This applies to us grown-ups too. Can you put your phone away during the bedtime routine? (The right answer is yes.) Just the presence of it—yes, even face down on the bookshelf—is distracting. Setting your own phone aside will help you be more present, and it models good habits. Plus, you'll probably sleep better yourself.

Use music. Music has a remarkable effect on children's bodies and brains, naturally lowering stress hormones and triggering the release of calming chemicals that help them feel safe and secure. When children hear gentle songs or lullabies at bedtime, their breathing and heart rates naturally slow to match the music's rhythm, bridging the gap from wakeful energy to rest time.

Making music a consistent part of your nightly routine takes advantage of this natural calming power. Over time, these musical cues automatically signal to the body that it's time to rest. It's like giving your child an emotional handrail to hold during bedtime.

Some practical ways to do this:

- **Sing to your child.** Your voice—regardless of how well you think you can or can't sing—has a uniquely soothing effect on your child. They find your voice's specific timbre inherently calming and associate it with safety and sleep. Start with something you know (it doesn't have to be a lullaby; it can be any mellow song you can think of), and as you get more comfortable, try to make up something on your own. Think of what you'd like to say to your child as they drift off to sleep ("I love you, Mama is here . . .") and try singing that. You might be surprised at what you come up with, and your child will love it.

- **Sing your instructions.** This reduces power struggles like you won't believe. When you sing "It's time to brush your teeth"—whether to a familiar tune or something you totally make up—instead of stating it, you shift the dynamic. Children are more likely to get on board because it not only gets their attention, but it feels like a game rather than an order.

- **Sing together.** When your child sings with you, they're actively participating in their own settling process without realizing it. Singing naturally regulates breathing since it requires taking deeper, more measured breaths, promoting relaxation. When you sing together, it strengthens your connection (literally, via the hormone oxytocin) and creates a sense of security. Plus, since singing requires attention to words and melody, it prevents your child's mind from racing, and can help distract from bedtime worries.

- **Keep it consistent.** The repetitive nature of songs is powerful. You might think you'll go out of your mind singing the same song over and over (my daughter had a phase with "Baa, Baa, Black Sheep" that felt like it lasted a decade), but each time children hear the familiar melody and rhythm, they're actually building stronger neural pathways for emotional regulation. The predictable structure helps them feel secure in knowing what comes next.

- **Develop a music routine.** Pick two or three special bedtime songs and use them in the same order each night. Here's an example:
  - Start with an upbeat, fun song; dance and wiggle and get the ya-yas out.
  - Sing a mellow "getting ready" song to the tune of "Twinkle, Twinkle, Little Star" while changing into jammies and brushing teeth.
  - Sing a quiet lullaby together when getting your child tucked into bed.

Remember, it's the consistency in this routine that matters, not your musical ability. You're not on TV. No judges here!

Create a soothing sensory environment. Designing a cozy, sensory-friendly bedtime experience is one hundred percent worth the effort. Essentially, you're making everything feel good to your child—particularly textures, sounds, and lights. This will be completely unique to your family, as children all have their own comfort quirks, and it may require a bit of trial and error, but it will pay off. Some things to try:

- A gentle back rub, foot massage, or light back scratch might feel calming and soothing to your child in the evening. This also gives them the gift of your undivided attention, which can feel just as good to them. Beyond helping them settle, this nurturing touch helps children develop body awareness and helps them tune in to what feels comforting to them.

  (My sister is one of those people who melts into complete relaxation with gentle touch. When we were kids, she'd lay her forearm, palm up, on my lap and say, "Scritchy scratch?" A light scratch would lull her to sleep in minutes.)

- Deep pressure can help soothe an anxious or overstimulated child. Make a calming "burrito" by gently but firmly wrapping your child in a soft blanket, as long as they're comfortable and can easily move if they want to. Weighted blankets can also be comforting to some children.

- What children see in the moments before sleep can influence how easily they drift off. Picture books with nature scenes like waves, clouds, or trees help create a peaceful sensory experience and are like a lullaby for the eyes, helping ease your child's busy mind. Research has actually shown that viewing images of nature, especially water, triggers our body's natural relaxation response.

  Dimming the lights for the bedtime routine, or having a special light that's just for bedtime, can be another visual signal that it's time to wind down.

- Adding peaceful sounds of nature, white noise, or even a fan can work great too. When we lived in New York City, in an apartment on upper Broadway (if you know, you know), the constant street noise was astounding. I finally found a white noise machine that became our nighttime hero. It created a cocoon of consistent, soothing sound that helped muffle the chaos below, and became such an essential part of my daughter's sleep routine that it traveled everywhere with us—she slept with it long after we moved away.

- Don't for a minute underestimate the power of super-soft bedding; it can work wonders, especially for children who are particular about textures. My older son waged a full-on rebellion against top sheets—he only wanted his ultra-soft blanket touching his skin, so I rolled with it. We now have lonely top sheets all over the house, but who cares—he was comfy and happy.

Gentle stretches. Easy, kid-friendly, yoga-inspired stretches can help release physical tension accumulated throughout the day. Some ideas:

- Rag Doll—Stand and slowly, gently flop forward like a puppet with its strings cut, arms dangling free. (Cooked spaghetti is another great visual.) Just let the upper body go, allowing the weight of the head to draw you closer to the ground. Take long breaths in and out.

- Cat and Cow—From a tabletop position on the floor, roll between arching your back (Cat) and dropping your belly (Cow). Meow! Moo! It's all part of it. Add in any other movements or stretches your child thinks an animal might make.

- Butterfly—Sit with the bottoms of the feet together and knees wide like wings. Nice and easy, let gravity do the work. Your child can flap their "wings," put their antennae on their head, and decide what color butterfly they want to be. (You should try this one too. It's excellent for releasing hip and lower back tension from the day.)

- Star—Lie flat on your back, stretching your arms and legs wide, making a star shape. Add tiny finger and toe wiggles and a smile to make your star twinkle. Sing the classic song. You can also start with "standing star" pose and transition slowly down to "sleepy star" on the floor.

Keep calm when it doesn't go to plan. While a consistent schedule matters, it's better to take an extra ten to fifteen minutes to maintain a peaceful bedtime routine than to rush and create tension. Your child will benefit more from a serene wind-down that runs a bit late than from strictly hitting the clock but sensing your stress about the time. Preserve the familiar sequence of your routine even if you're running behind schedule.

This makes it even more important to take care of yourself during the day as best you can. If you've carved out a few quiet moments to yourself, you won't feel (as) resentful if the you-know-what hits the fan and your post-bedtime me-time gets cut short.

Share moments of joy, wins, and gratitude. A nightly practice of exchanging happy moments, small victories, or simple thank-yous is a powerful way to strengthen the bond with your child. As a bonus, it helps teach them gratitude and optimism. Here are a few ideas to try—choose one that feels good to you, or blend a few together:

- Share some wins. Take a moment at bedtime to share something that went well today, whether it was for you or someone else—maybe your older child got the part they wanted in the school play! Total win. Then invite your child to share one too. A simple practice of celebrating victories, no matter how small they are, helps your child look for positivity in everyday moments. And when you celebrate others' successes together, you're showing them that joy multiplies when it's shared—helping them develop empathy.
- Exchange compliments. Share one genuine, positive observation about who your child is at their core, focusing on a character strength ("You are . . ."), like, "You're so kind and helpful when your friends need you." Then invite them to share what they notice about you. This sweet exchange helps your child feel proud of who they truly are, not just what they do.
- Chat about your highlights. Take turns talking about one of your favorite parts of the day. You might tell your child (briefly) about an

exciting project at work or a funny conversation with a friend (showing them that you're a whole person with your own joys), or it could be a moment you and your child shared together. Then let your child tell you about their own highlight. Sometimes this is quite illuminating, especially when you find out that after the long-planned and expensive trip to the children's museum, their high point of the day was the snack from the vending machine.

- Tell a silly joke. Humor is an awesome way to create a positive association with sleep routines. It defuses tension and is another way to strengthen your bond during what can be a tough transition time. When you both giggle over a funny face or share a goofy joke, you're creating positive associations with bedtime rituals. This can become a cherished part of the routine. (My favorite silly joke for littles: "Knock-knock." "Who's there?" "Impatient cow." "Impatient c— " "MOOO!")
- Express gratitude. Say a few thank-yous—it could be as simple as asking your child to name one person they'd like to thank from the day. ("I want to thank the bus driver for taking me to school. Thank you!") Then you share yours as well. Quick and easy. These few minutes of sharing gratitude help both of you notice the good stuff, even on hard days.

Mama Mantra

Small joys create a life.

Bring in the family. Being the only person who can get your child to sleep is exhausting and unsustainable, and can leave you feeling trapped. Ideally, your bedtime routine is consistent and effective enough that any trusted loved one can be relatively successful at getting your child to sleep. Making bedtime a shared family responsibility—easier said than done, I know—is important: it prevents your child from becoming totally dependent on you for bedtime. Plus, it enables you to go out once in a while and be a Grown-Up Person.

If you have other children, consider bringing them into the mix as well. Having an older child read to their younger sibling makes for some pretty sweet moments and can become a part of the day that your child really looks forward to. It will strengthen their sibling connection while helping everyone wind down. Double win.

Create anticipation. The way we approach bedtime significantly influences how our children experience it. When we sigh heavily and say to our partner, "See you in an hour or so, I guess, I have to do bedtime," children pick up on this energy and can push back—who wants to feel like a chore?

If you can, try viewing bedtime as an opportunity to be present and close with your child. Use positive language, creating moments to look forward to. As the end of the day approaches, highlight upcoming parts of the routine with something like enthusiasm: "Tonight we'll get to read that new story together!" or "I can't wait for our sleepy stretches, my body really needs them." This shift in language from "have to" to "get to" helps children associate bedtime with connection rather than separation. When children know they can count on these meaningful moments with you, bedtime becomes less about saying goodbye (cueing the separation anxiety) and more about sharing a peaceful close to the day.

If you work outside the home, bedtime can be especially meaningful—these moments might be some of the only one-on-one time you get with your child all day. Rather than rushing through it—even though I know you're tired too—try to embrace the evening as a chance to connect and share special time.

Your attitude sets the tone. When you genuinely look forward to this time together, your child will too. And if you're still dreading it, no matter how hard you try? Fake it till you make it, as they say.

Stay in your lane: trust what works for your family. Don't let your mom friends or your father-in-law or anyone else dictate what works best for you and your child. What works beautifully for one family's bedtime routine might be totally ineffective—or even counterproductive—for another.

Case in point: everybody and their uncle advised me to give my daughter a warm bath before bed to settle her down (see above: epic sleep troubles). Hilarious! She took it as an opportunity to ramp up her energy level to an eleven out of ten, and whenever possible escaped the bathroom to run naked around the house, flinging bubbles everywhere and screaming like a banshee. So for us, no bedtime baths.

(I can hear your concern: Did she still get bathed regularly? Not really, no. She's grown up now, though, and showers daily.)

Calm Starts with You

Post-dinner, pre-bedtime: your shoulders are tight, your patience is wearing thin, and bedtime looms. And when your child is finally asleep, then you get to come back downstairs and do the dishes! Hooray . . .

These quick exercises are your lifeline. They're fast, simple ways to reset—no meditation cushion required. Just practical tools to help you navigate the final stretch of the day with something like presence and calm.

Shoulder Squeeze

Are you a shoulder-tenser like I am? Our shoulders often carry our accumulated tension from stressors of all kinds. This simple exercise creates an intentional cycle of tension and release, helping drain away the day's stored stress. The mindful drop of your shoulders signals to your body that it's time to transition out of "doing" mode and toward winding down. It's simple to do anywhere, seated or standing.

HOW-TO

Sit or stand tall and slowly squeeze your shoulders up toward your ears. Feel the tension building.

Hold, squeezing tightly, for a few seconds. Inhale.

Slowly exhale and release, letting your shoulders drop completely down. Feel those muscles relax.

Repeat as many times as you'd like.

You might want to bring to mind a particularly stressful thing that happened today—really focus on it as you squeeze your shoulders up—and then intentionally let it go.

Tiny Good Things

When your day has been about a week long, it can be hard to feel even remotely optimistic, especially as everyone gets tired, including you. This gentle practice isn't about forcing positivity or dismissing the very real hard parts of daily life with young children. It's about noticing that, no matter how challenging it was today, tiny specks of goodness were also present. Taking a few mindful breaths creates space to hold both.

HOW-TO

Sitting, standing, or lying down, take a few long breaths in, and long breaths out.

With each exhale, let your body soften.

Bring to mind one tiny good thing from today.

It could be as small as the warmth of your morning coffee in your hands, your child's sleepy smile when they woke up, or the kind exchange you had with the cashier at the store.

Take another deep breath, holding this small bit of joy in your mind.

If you can, let it connect to one or two more tiny good things. Let each one sit with you for a few breaths.

Done Is Better Than Perfect

Was your child fed, kept warm and safe, and loved today? Did the basics get taken care of? Then all is well. It probably wasn't perfect, but perfect is overrated, not to mention unattainable. You showed up, worked hard, tried. That's enough.

Try this to help let go of those "shoulds." Tomorrow's a new day.

HOW-TO

Get yourself comfy and close your eyes if you want to. Take a long breath in and let it out, relaxing your body.

Picture all the "shoulds" that are lingering in your mind: "I should have replied to that email," "I should have been more patient," "I should have finished that project"–whatever they are for you.

Imagine gathering all of these "shoulds" into a delicate bubble floating before you. Let it hold the endless mental list.

Take a long breath in, and with your next exhale, gently blow that bubble into the evening sky. Watch it drift away, carrying those "shoulds" with it.

Now picture everything you did today. I'm guessing it was about two thousand things. Envision the meals made, the hugs given, the snacks doled out, the tasks completed.

Take another deep breath and acknowledge the truth: You showed up today. You did your best. That's plenty.

Mama Mantra

Done is better than perfect.

Connection Activities

Watch me demonstrate all of these Good Night activities, songs, and rhythm games, plus get the playlist, right here!

Here are some simple mindfulness activities that honor your child's natural rhythms. These kid-friendly approaches keep the focus on comfort and calm while embracing your child's totally normal desire for imaginative play and movement at the end of the day. Building these practices into your routine now sets the foundation for joyful connection at bedtime and will pay off in the years to come.

IN THE CLASSROOM: These activities are also perfect for quiet time, helping students transition from active learning to a calmer, more centered state before storytime, silent reading, or rest.

Bear Breath

Busy bodies calm down fast when they pretend to be sleepy bears taking long breaths in and out, snug in their caves. If your child needs help settling, let them bear-crawl around first, gathering pretend berries and fish to fill their bellies before curling up in their "cave" to rest.

SONG PAIRING: "All Tucked In"

SCRIPT

Pretend you're a bear, hibernating for the winter. You can be any kind of bear you want.

When bears hibernate, they breathe slooowly, in and out through their noses.

First, find your cozy cave and get really comfy.

Now take a long breath in through your nose, and let it all the way out.

Take another long breath in through your nose, and let it all the way out.

Feel how cozy, safe, and warm you are in your bear cave.

Take one more really long, slow breath in through your nose, and let it all the way out.

(*Repeat the breaths for as long as you like.*)

Sleepy Mouse

For a child, curling up like a tiny mouse in its nest creates the soothing sensation of being safe and protected; the gentle forward fold naturally slows breathing and quiets busy minds and bodies. This one can be done on the floor or on your child's bed.

SONG PAIRING: "Just Be"

SCRIPT

Sit on your heels, fold your body forward, and put your head down on the floor.

Curl up into a little ball, just like a tiny mouse.

Breathe in, and breathe out.
Slowly . . . breathe in, and breathe out.
Even more slowly . . . breathe in, and breathe out.
Let your whole body relax.
Such a sleepy little mouse you are!
Stay here as long as you want.

Rhythm & Rhyme Time

Part chant, part affirmation, this gentle rhyme combines calming breathwork with reassuring repetition. Keep a steady, slow beat and say it as many times as you like. You can pick just one verse to repeat, or do all three.

Shake Off the Day

I shake off the day
I let it fly away
I put my hands on my heart and I breathe.

I let it all go
I let it all be
I put my hands on my heart and I breathe.

I did my best
Now it's time to rest
I put my hands on my heart and I breathe.

Scrunch and Let Go

This is a child-friendly version of progressive muscle relaxation, a simple and super-effective tool for releasing pent-up energy and tension. It helps children calm and relax their bodies. It's ideal to do when your child is cozy in their bed, so when they relax they're already in the right place for sleep.

 **SONG PAIRING:** "When You Sleep"

SCRIPT

Time for Scrunch and Let Go!
First, stretch your body out long.
Now scrunch up your toes, and make all the muscles in your legs really strong.
Pull your belly in, and squeeze the muscles in your arms.
Make your hands into fists, and scrunch up your face.
If you want to, squeeze your eyes shut.
Squeeze all your muscles super tight!
Hold them really tight!
Now take a long breath in, and as you let the air out, slowly let all those muscles go.
Take another long breath in, and as you let the air out, let your whole body relax. Aaahhhh . . .
(*Repeat as necessary–sometimes a few rounds are needed!*)

Rhythm & Rhyme Time

This sweet rhyme uses the familiar, cozy experience of cooling down a cup of hot chocolate to encourage long, deep breaths, turning a calming mindfulness practice into a playful game.

Hot Cocoa

(*Hold your cup of pretend hot cocoa in front of you. Say the rhyme to a steady, slow beat.*)

Mmm, hot cocoa
it's my favorite treat!
Mmm, hot cocoa
so tasty and so sweet!
If it's too hot, I know what to do
Long, deep breaths
That will help it cool . . .

(*Take a few long breaths in and out, blowing gently on your "cocoa" to cool it off. When you're ready, say the rest of the rhyme.*)

Mmm, hot cocoa
I take a little sip (*Make a slurpy sound.*)
Mmm, hot cocoa
I'll drink up every bit!

Candle Breath

This gentle, focused activity guides children to breathe deeply as they envision their imaginary candle flame dancing and wiggling. The playful concept keeps their attention, and the long, slow breaths are soothing and calming.

**SONG PAIRING:** "I Have a Light"

SCRIPT

Imagine you're holding a candle.

Take a long breath in, and slowly, gently blow the air out toward your candle.

You want to make your candle flame wiggle, but . . . don't blow it out!

Long breath in, slooow breath out.

Long breath in, slooow breath out.

See the candle flame dance and wiggle in your mind.

Long breath in, slooow breath out.

Long breath in, slooow breath out.

Long breath in . . . now gently . . . blow your candle out!

The Worry Box

I did this with my youngest at bedtime for years, and it was magical. Your child can put all their worries into a pretend box so they don't have to carry anxiety in their minds. It's not about fixing anything—it's about lightening their mental load, helping them feel calmer and more peaceful so they can rest.

**SONG PAIRING:** "No More Worries"

SCRIPT

Imagine you have a little box in your hand.

It will hold all your worries so you can have a good rest.

Do you have a worry?

Say it out loud.
Then put it into the box.
Do you have another worry?
Say it out loud.
Then put it into the box.
Say all your worries out loud.
They can be big worries, or they can be small worries.
Put them all into the box.
Now put the top on tight!
Put the box somewhere safe, or let me hold it for you.
You don't have to think about those worries now.
You can rest.

Together Time: Partner Connection Activity

Starfish

This gentle finger-tracing exercise creates a soothing moment of focused connection between you and your child. The slow, deliberate movement combined with deep breaths naturally calms both of you, while the visual of imagining a sparkly starfish makes it fun. Make it easy and extra mellow by simply playing the song and following along with the lyrics.

 **SONG PAIRING:** "Peaceful and Calm"

HOW-TO

Sit facing each other, or sit on or near your child's bed once they're tucked in—close enough that you can easily reach each other's hands.

Hold your "starfish" (one of your hands) out toward your child with your palm facing them. Have them use their pointer finger to trace up your thumb while you both take a long breath in. As they trace down, slowly breathe out.

Have your child continue tracing up and down each of your fingers—up on the inhale, down on the exhale.

When they finish tracing all five fingers, switch roles so you trace your child's "starfish." Take your time tracing all five fingers, matching the breathing to the gentle movement.

Remind your child that they can trace their own "starfish" to feel peaceful and calm anytime they want to.

Finish by placing your palms against your child's palms and holding still for just a moment.

Good Night Playlist

"All Tucked In"

Invites children to imagine they're sleepy baby animals tucked into their cozy beds.

"Just Be"

A soothing melody, warm and peaceful.

"When You Sleep"

A layered a cappella lullaby that weaves a serene bedtime vibe.

"I Have a Light"

A gentle, meditative round that weaves a cocoon of calm perfect for rest time.

"No More Worries"

Dreamy and calming, allowing children to put their worries aside so they can rest.

"Peaceful and Calm"

A rhythmic melody that guides children through slow, mindful breathing, creating a soothing bridge to sleep.

Your Turn

Create the Peaceful Bedtime You Both Deserve

Here's what I wish someone had told me during those three years of bedtime disasters: you don't have to accept nightly chaos as just "the way it is." (I don't know about you, but I really don't like that phrase.) The tips and tools in this chapter give you the power to transform your evening routine from something you dread into a process you both actually enjoy—and when you use them consistently, you're creating a lot more than just a path to sleep for your child. You're building a foundation of trust and emotional safety that they'll carry with them long after they've outgrown bedtime stories.

Think about what becomes possible when bedtime flows peacefully: evenings where your child looks forward to winding down with you, routines so solid that other family members can step in successfully, sweet rituals where you both reflect on the day, sharing small joys.

You have the tools and the power to decide what bedtime feels like in your home. Will it be an hour (or more) of resistance and negotiation, or will it be the sweet close to each day where you and your child reconnect after being apart? Do you want to spend your evenings feeling frazzled and trapped, or confident and present?

The choice is yours, and you now have everything you need to create exactly the kind of peaceful, joyful bedtime you and your child both deserve.

When you use these Calm & Connect steps, you'll Create:

More of This

Self-care that allows you to be present

Peaceful connection time that you both look forward to

A consistent routine that works for your family

A cozy bedtime vibe with soothing sensory elements

Trust in what works for your child

Moments of gratitude and shared joy

Less of That

The feeling that bedtime is something you have to survive

Sole responsibility for getting your child to sleep

Bedtime dread

Comparison or worry about what others think

Negotiations and power struggles

The rush to stay on a strict evening schedule

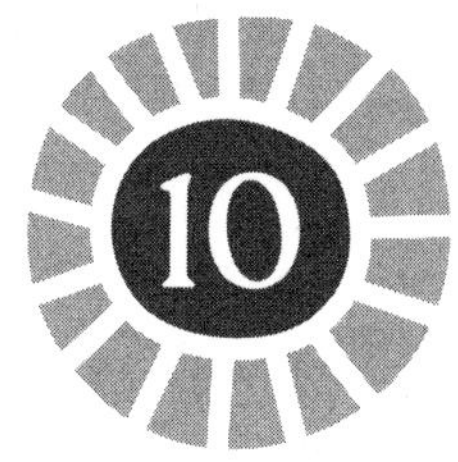

SOS

Your First Aid Kit for Big Feelings

DURING THE MORE THAN two decades that I have been a parent, I may have experienced every kind of kid meltdown: I've fireman-carried my hollering child out of the grocery store, gone toe-to-toe with an incensed toddler screaming "Why won't you help me?" in my face at 2 AM, and talked our preschool's director off the ledge after my son angrily bit her daughter. (Somehow, we weren't kicked out of that school.)

I can tell you with certainty that tantrums are part of life with young children no matter what. So, while this book primarily focuses on creating mindful moments of connection with your little ones during calmer times, I've dedicated this chapter to those inevitable tough moments. Here you'll find practical tools to help you both move through your child's intense emotions in the healthiest way you can. Hopefully, this means with a bit less drama and a bit more grace and compassion.

Here's another thing I'm sure of: your child's tantrums and outbursts are not only inevitable but normal; in fact, they're developmentally necessary. Children are born fully equipped to feel the full range of human emotions (and with stunning intensity), but have exactly zero skills to manage, process, or navigate these feelings. This fundamental mismatch—big feelings, tiny coping skills—creates the perfect scenario for emotional eruptions. It's like a jet engine on a paper airplane. Their brains are literally under construction, with the rational, problem-solving parts developing years after the emotional center is up and running at full throttle.

The key is to recognize these moments for what they are: desperate attempts by your child to deal with overwhelming feelings like frustration, disappointment, and anger. They have to learn how to deal with these emotions—and unfortunately, the only way out is through, as they say. I'm not suggesting that you should welcome tantrums with open arms, but getting some perspective on them can be very helpful. When you view these outbursts as essential learning opportunities—milestones in your child's development—rather than as parenting failures or something about your child that needs to be fixed, you create space for both you and your child to grow. These challenging moments, as messy and loud as they may be, are where emotional intelligence starts to develop.

The Power of Your Calm

Your ability to remain calm and centered isn't just helpful here—it's the single most powerful factor in determining how these moments unfold. Indeed, how grounded you stay in the heat of the moment fundamentally shapes its outcome. Think of your child like a tiny boat in a big storm, getting whipped this way and that in the wind and waves. You're the boat's sturdy anchor, holding steady and strong no matter how big those waves get. Your capacity to stay anchored transforms the entire situation.

And it's probably the hardest part of parenting.

Not to mention: Do crises usually happen when you're well rested, patient, and feeling your best? Of course not. No, they ambush you when you're running late, sleep-deprived, or at the tail end of your own long, hard day. Plus, our nervous systems are highly attuned to our children's distress. When they lose it, our bodies instinctively respond—heart racing, muscles tensing, stress hormones flooding our system. It's not easy to stay calm and steady, but that's exactly the goal.

Our job in a meltdown situation is, in short, to keep it together. We need to maintain our composure in order to be a source of support and modeling for our child. During a child's spiral, the steady presence of a parent who is calm and regulated works wonders.

Our job is NOT to end a tantrum or outburst, to stop it in its tracks, or to make it go away as quickly as possible. That's not healthy or productive for our child or for our relationship with them.

Childhood is essentially Big Feelings Boot Camp; storms are inevitable. Our job isn't to prevent the storms but to help our children learn they can survive them—so that eventually, when they're grown (sniff), they'll remember our steady presence and find that same steadiness within themselves.

What If . . .

Imagine approaching your child's next meltdown armed with practical tools that help both of you navigate the storm. What if their meltdown didn't derail you too? Picture yourself remaining centered when chaos erupts, using simple techniques that actually work in the moment. It's about having enough mindful practices in your back pocket that, when emotions overflow, you're not left empty-handed. And while practice doesn't make perfect here, it makes it a little better every time.

And here's something that might sound surprising: these challenging moments, when weathered together, can actually deepen your connection with your child. Some of my most profound bonds with my kids formed in the aftermath of our toughest emotional storms. The trust that's built when you remain stable and centered in the face of chaos is powerful.

What you'll find in the following pages are strategies to keep yourself grounded when the emotional lightning strikes, because the least helpful thing we can do when our children are losing it is join them in the chaos. Think of this chapter as your emergency toolkit for those moments when your child has gone full tornado mode. Some of these tools will work brilliantly for your family, others won't fit. That's as it should be; we're all different, and we're all works in progress.

Setting the Stage: Tips for Keeping Your Cool

When your child starts melting down—whether it's a full-on tantrum in the hardware store or a breakdown at bedtime—what you do next matters. The way you respond to your child's powerful emotions now builds the foundation for how they'll handle their disappointments and challenges down the road. The following tips will help you keep your cool when your child is losing theirs, prioritize what's important, and come out the other side with the relationship between you and your child not just intact, but even stronger.

Safety first, period. When a child is having a meltdown, safety is the highest priority—for your child, for yourself, and for anyone else around. A child's rational thinking is basically offline in these moments, and their body is likely in a fight-or-flight state, making them capable of doing things they wouldn't normally do. Your number one job is to create a physically safe environment by removing anything that could be dangerous, preventing them from hurting anyone or hurting themselves, and if you can, moving to a quiet area with as little stimulation as possible (think dim light and soft surfaces).

Stay calm and maintain firm physical boundaries when necessary, using simple language like, "I'm going to help your body move to a safe place." Make clear that it's not OK to hurt anyone. It doesn't matter one bit where you are or who's watching as you haul your child like a sack of potatoes from the restaurant/museum/in-laws' living room while everyone pretends not to stare. Safety beats social decorum every time; your parental dignity will recover.

Remember, the heightened emotions might make the situation feel like an emergency—it certainly does to your child—but it's not. Keep it together. Your firm and steady presence provides the container your child needs until their storm passes.

Prioritize connection. Once safety is established, connection is your priority over anything else. The groceries melting in the car, that email you were about to send, all of it can wait. Connection can mean sitting next to your child and breathing deeply while they sob or rage—which may feel like doing nothing, but it's actually doing something profound and powerful: your groundedness is showing them that you won't abandon them or freak out when things get hard, and that your love and presence aren't conditional on their behavior. Stay in it, stay calm, and trust that they will eventually co-regulate—meaning calm down because they see you calm—with you.

Remember that you're the sturdy anchor of your child's tiny, wind-whipped boat, and you're holding steady and strong in the fury. There's no need to talk much, if at all, unless it's a simple repeated phrase like "I'm here." Your composure speaks volumes in these moments.

Mama Mantra

I am their safe space.

Acknowledge their wants. Simple validation of your child's feelings is your secret weapon—even when you think what they want is unreasonable or maybe even totally bonkers.

Say your child demands an ice cream cone and you say no; the protesting and crying starts and quickly escalates. Instead of immediately shutting them down (your instinct to make the crying stop) or giving in just to put an end to it (also very tempting), try this: "I get that you're disappointed. We're not getting ice cream today."

You haven't promised anything or changed your stance. You've just recognized that what they want is very real to them. In moments of distress, children need to feel connected to you, not pushed away. When you acknowledge their feelings, your child feels seen and heard. The volume of their crying probably won't drop immediately, or certainly not as fast as you'd like, but you've created a tiny bridge of connection—and that's what helps them eventually get back to being able to manage themselves.

When you say, "Stop crying, you're not getting ice cream," it feels dismissive to a child and usually backfires, often escalating the meltdown. We want them to be able to manage their emotions, right? When we command them to stop crying, we're not showing them how—and we're also inadvertently teaching them we're not comfortable with their big feelings.

Telling them to stop being upset also misses the opportunity to help them manage disappointment. Think about it: if you don't let your child work through their frustration about ice cream today, how will they learn to manage the inevitable setbacks that will come later in life—not getting picked for the team, or a job not working out?

All of this is to say: don't change your mind about the ice cream cone. This requires superhuman patience and will. But in those moments when you validate their big emotions instead of dismissing them, you're helping them develop the emotional intelligence they'll need throughout their lives.

Mama Mantra

Respond, don't react.

Don't "fix it." When your child is in emotional crisis, resist the urge to immediately jump into solution mode. By rushing to solve the problem, we unknowingly send the message that our child's feelings are inconvenient, something to be quickly "fixed."

Your child needs to feel seen and supported; sitting with them as they navigate their upset or anger rather than rushing to change or fix anything shows them that difficult emotions are manageable. Let them make their way through their feelings with your steady support before moving toward solutions.

They're not ready to think about problem-solving anyway—remember that children in the midst of big emotions aren't in a rational state. Trying to reason your way out of this tough moment is like attempting a thoughtful conversation with someone who's underwater.

If you've messed up, say you're sorry. When you lose your cool with your child—whether you yelled or spoke harshly in a moment of frustration—apologize. Children deserve the same respect we'd give anyone else when we've hurt them, and apologizing models the accountability we want them to develop themselves. A proper apology means acknowledging what you did without excuses ("I'm sorry I yelled when you spilled your soup. That wasn't OK, and you didn't deserve that") and making a clear commitment to do better ("Next time I feel really frustrated, I'm going to take a deep breath before I do anything").

Just as important is understanding what a real apology is NOT. It's not "I'm sorry if you felt hurt" (which questions the validity of their feelings) or "I'm sorry, but I'm doing everything myself here" (which is making excuses for your behavior). A genuine apology doesn't include "if" or "but."

These words undermine your accountability and teach children that apologizing is about deflecting responsibility rather than owning it. (I feel so strongly about this—if there's one thing my kids know, it's how to apologize properly.)

I can't stress enough how valuable this repair process is to your child and to your relationship with them. Not only does it show your child that you admit your mistakes rather than defend them, it gives them permission to be imperfect. They learn that when we make mistakes, we take responsibility—and then we move forward with grace and self-compassion.

Do what you need to do to get through it. Sometimes you're in survival mode, and your usual rules just don't apply. That's OK. In those moments, what matters most isn't keeping up your perfect parenting standards—it's meeting basic needs, maintaining your strong connection with your child, and getting through it. Sometimes that means screen time rules go out the window during a particularly trying day, or that you let them fall asleep in your bed because you simply cannot face another evening battle.

When my son was little and recovering from a nasty illness, he refused to eat. Consumed with worry, I offered all the gentle, healthy options I could think of. He finally lost it, his little body rigid with frustration, screaming that he wouldn't eat that, or that, or that. My grandmother calmly pulled out a package of cream cheese, made some into a ball, rolled it in chocolate chips, and offered it to him. (True story.) As one of those bonkers-about-nutrition moms at the time, I was not happy about this one bit, but I kept my mouth shut. He gobbled it up—and then he ate something else, and something else. And despite my fear that he'd request cream cheese truffles at every meal going forward, it didn't come up again. That was that.

Adapting as you need to when you're in survival mode doesn't mean you're not doing a good job. It means that you're smart enough to know when to bend so you don't break, and that you're giving yourself and your child grace during a really hard time.

Another quick story (I have plenty of "survival mode" tales): there was a time in her young life that my daughter simply would not sleep, and my exhaustion brought me to my knees. During a visit to the pediatrician, I asked her yet again which sleep training method I should try next or what book held the answer. The doctor looked at me, taking in my unwashed hair and the bags under my eyes, and said, "What you need is to get some sleep. Would she sleep with you?" (I must have nodded; it's pretty fuzzy in my memory.) "Then that's what you do, for now."

"For now" were the words I needed to hear. I wasn't going back on my policy that she was too old to sleep with us (or giving in to my worry that she'd still be in our bed when she was in high school). We brought her into our bed, and we all slept. It was amazing. And it was temporary. That rest gave me the capacity to regroup and figure out what to do next (and yes, she transitioned back to her own bed just fine).

In survival mode, focus on the core needs that matter most: safety, health, and connection. Let go of the guilt. You're not dropping the ball—you're adapting to challenging circumstances in which there are no good solutions. When the crisis eventually passes (and it will), just return to your usual routines without lengthy explanations to your child. Don't make a big deal about it. You're actually demonstrating the kind of resilience and problem-solving we all want our children to learn.

Listen. What your upset child needs far more than your words is for you to just listen to them. Save the teachable moment for later. You're not in a teachable moment anyway—remember that the part of their brain that can learn things is currently not functioning.

I know you're dying to ask all the questions—When did the upsetting thing happen? What did the fifth grader say to you exactly? Did the teacher hear it? But the best thing you can do right now is zip it. Those details can wait. While your natural instinct as a parent is to get all the information and/or offer solutions, what actually helps your child feel better is knowing you're fully in it with them.

I'll share two simple phrases that I've found have made a huge difference in these types of situations. The first phrase I live by to this day: "What else?"

When your child is flooded with emotion, resist the urge to interrupt with questions or ideas of your own. Instead, once they've shared the initial problem, gently ask "What else?" and then wait. And wait some more.

Make the space—however much they need—for them to share in their own way, on their own timeline. Let them tell it all, get it all out. Don't interrupt, ask questions, or even show much of a reaction. Your patience—even if you're sitting in the most uncomfortable position ever or desperately need to pee—gives them permission to fully express what's bothering them. Often what first comes out isn't the real issue anyway—that tends to just be the thing that put them over the edge. It's usually what follows, after they feel truly heard, that reveals what's really going on.

Mama Mantra

Wait and listen.

The second phrase I use, and only when I feel they might be truly ready to answer, is "What do you need right now?"

This simple question shifts the focus from the problem to potential support. Again, it's not about fixing the situation that caused their tantrum; it's supporting them in this moment of big upset. It tells your child that your priority is helping them. It also gently guides them to look inward and develop awareness of their own needs—whether that's a hug, a drink of water, or their favorite teddy.

Side note: while I'm all for emotional awareness, young children don't necessarily need to "name it to tame it" right away. Don't push them prematurely into identifying or labeling their emotions—that can sometimes feel like pressure when they're still overwhelmed. Young children experience emotions more as bodily sensations than as clearly defined feelings. Focus on comfort and on meeting their needs in the moment.

These two simple phrases—"What else?" and "What do you need right now?"—can help create a foundation of trust that lets your child know they'll always be heard and that you'll always be there to support them exactly as they are.

Calm Starts with You

The most powerful parenting tool you have in moments of chaos is your own regulated nervous system. These quick mindful exercises are practical tools you can use anytime, anywhere. They're designed for real-life situations, like when your toddler is in a category-five meltdown at the park or bedtime has become a showdown. They'll help shift your emotional state from overwhelmed to resourceful.

Taking thirty seconds to reset doesn't mean you're checking out; it means you're consciously creating space between trigger and reaction—

this is where your best parenting lives. When your child's emotions are too big for their body, they need you to hold steady. These small moments of mindful awareness help you become the anchor they're searching for in their storm.

The Invisible Shield

Your child needs you to witness their distress, not get swept up in it alongside them. Absorbing their big feelings only means two people are now overwhelmed instead of one. Creating a mental boundary might feel like withholding compassion or empathy, but it's the opposite: it's preserving your own steady center so you can offer genuine support—rather than reactive anxiety—from a calm place.

When you feel yourself getting caught up in your child's emotions, this quick visualization helps establish an emotional boundary without disconnecting from your child and what they're going through.

HOW-TO

Take a full breath in and let it out.

Imagine a transparent shield or bubble around your body.

This shield doesn't separate you from your child, but it filters the intensity of what's happening outside.

Take another full breath in and let it out.

Visualize the shield protecting you from getting caught up in the high emotions happening around you.

Silently tell yourself: "I can be present and compassionate without absorbing all of this energy."

Remember this shield keeps your calm and steady self intact, preventing you from overreacting to the intense emotions your child is experiencing.

Protected by your shield, you can now respond to your child's needs with tenderness and compassion.

Bathroom Break

When emotions are running high, a brief physical separation might be necessary in order to not lose your mama marbles. This strategy only works when your child is physically safe and you've clearly communicated your return ("Mommy needs exactly thirty seconds and then I will be back"). It's a quick reset that does wonders to transform a spiraling situation for both of you into one you can manage with relative equilibrium.

HOW-TO

Ensure your child is safe. Tell them you'll be back in thirty seconds. Make sure you're back in thirty seconds.

Step into the bathroom and close the door.

Place both hands on the counter or sink. Focus on the cool sensation.

Look at yourself in the mirror with kindness.

Take a few slow breaths in and out.

If it might feel good, splash cold water on your wrists or face.

Remind yourself: "I can handle this." (Or use a Mama Mantra of your choice.)

Take one more long breath in and out.

Return to your child, repeating your mantra silently to yourself as needed.

Time Traveler

I remember thinking that my fellow shoppers at the grocery store would be talking about my child's epic checkout line meltdown for days. Been there? Every parent has, no matter how judgmental the gawkers might seem in the moment—even though they've almost certainly been in your exact shoes.

This simple mental shift helps you reclaim perspective amid the chaos—because despite how it feels right now, this episode will soon be just a short blip on your family's timeline. (Maybe it will even become part of hilarious family lore, like when I wheeled my screaming child out of the store in someone's empty cart, abandoning my own cart full of food. So funny now, SO awful then.)

It helps you realize moments like these are par for the course in raising young children. You're not alone.

HOW-TO

Ensure your child is safe. Take a long breath in and out.

In your mind, fast-forward one hour from now—picture where you'll be, what you'll be doing.

Take another breath, then imagine tonight at bedtime.

Visualize tomorrow morning, with a new day's fresh start.

Now picture next week, when this moment will be just a distant memory.

One more long breath in and out, bringing yourself back to the present moment.

Notice how you feel with this wider perspective.

Remind yourself that these intense moments are just a small dot on the timeline of just one day.

Bring your attention back to your child, reminding yourself that this will pass.

Four-Beat Mantra

This simple exercise engages your body and mind together—as you touch each finger to your thumb, the gentle pressure points give your brain something physical to focus on, helping you remain calm in a heated moment.

The rhythmic movement creates a soothing pattern that helps quiet your nervous system. And by combining the movement with calming words, you're keeping your brain busy enough that it can't spiral into stressed-out thoughts.

HOW-TO

Any four-syllable phrase works. Let's use "I can do this" as an example.

Start by touching your index finger to your thumb. Say (out loud or silently) "I."

Touch your middle finger to your thumb. Say "can."

Touch your ring finger to your thumb. Say "do."

And touch your pinkie to your thumb. Say "this."

That's it. Repeat.

The rhythm should be steady and deliberate, maybe even matching your breathing, if that feels natural. Repeat as many times as you like.

Here are some suggestions for four-beat mantras, or come up with your own.

I am here now.

I am patient.

This too will pass.

I am centered.

I am present.

I love ______________________. *(Fill in your child's name.)*

Soothing Connection Strategies

After nearly two decades of navigating the big emotions of my own children and working with many others, I've learned powerful regulation strategies that have helped soothe countless tantrums and breakdowns. Some came from collaborations with wonderful occupational therapists and educators who shared their evidence-based approaches, others from simple trial and error in my own home.

Present these strategies—and only one at a time, please—as gentle offerings of support. Avoid asking a lot of questions that could overwhelm your child further: "Do you want your blanket? Should we go outside? How about something to drink?" is all too much to process for an already dysregulated child. Instead, put helpful options within reach, saying simply: "There's an ice pack if you want it."

Lastly, keep in mind that a technique that soothes your child one day might frustrate them the next. (Saying things like, "But this is your favorite bear!"—not helpful.) The goal is to give support while honoring their choices, with the understanding that calming strategies for a child can vary wildly from moment to moment.

Model long, deep breaths. Working with the breath is one of the most powerful stress regulators there is—and it's always available, wherever you are. When your child is in a full spiral, though, suggesting they take a deep breath is like telling the wind to stop blowing. I don't know about you, but when someone tells me to take a deep breath when I'm angry, it just irritates me even more.

A child who's already overwhelmed will struggle to follow your directions and might get more upset. But what you can do is model: sit near your upset child and begin taking slow, audible breaths yourself. Make them visible—put a hand on your heart or belly as you breathe in deeply, then exhale slowly. Don't ask them to join you or even acknowledge what you're doing.

Your child's nervous system is designed to attune to yours. Even when they seem completely unreachable, they'll unconsciously begin to match your breathing patterns, and this co-regulation can be very powerful. The stealth approach of modeling near your child accomplishes two things: Your child's breathing will naturally slow to match yours in the moment, helping them calm down without even realizing it. And with repetition, they'll also eventually internalize this strategy for when they need it down the road.

This is a perfect example of why it's so important to practice mindful activities during calm moments, so that they're tools at the ready when a crisis comes. Then they can be pulled out at the first signs of frustration, helping soothe a meltdown or—imagine—maybe preventing it altogether. When exercises like Bear Breath (page 170) and Hot Cocoa (page 173) have become familiar favorites, your child's body already knows what deep breathing feels like. Their muscles and nervous system recognize the patterns, even when their thinking brain is offline during a meltdown. It's like creating a path through the woods before you need it—when you're lost, that familiar trail is already there.

Get moving. Big emotions need somewhere to go. Children's bodies innately understand this, even though they can't articulate it. Physical movement creates a natural pathway for all of that emotional energy to move and be processed. When children are overwhelmed by feelings, movement helps them discharge some of the emotional intensity and bring them back to a calmer state.

Some children instinctively seek something called proprioceptive input—pressure or resistance that helps them feel where their body is in space—through activities like jumping, crashing into pillows, or bear hugs when emotions start feeling too big to contain. Others like soothing motion: when my son was young and overwhelmed, he often asked to go for a drive in the car. The gentle rocking and forward motion created a predictable, soothing sensory experience that helped his body downshift and begin to relax.

Here are some movement ideas to try:

- Rhythmic bouncing on your lap
- Rocking (on your lap or in a rocking chair)
- Going for a drive
- Drumming (a bucket or pot works fine)

- Strong bear hugs
- Swinging
- Running or walking outside
- Jumping into a pile of pillows
- Pushing against a wall
- Pounding a cushion, couch, or pillow
- Self-hugs with "butterfly taps" (arms crossed, tapping each shoulder)
- Animal walks (stomping like a dinosaur, jumping like a kangaroo)

No amount of "use your words" helps in high-intensity moments—and if the storm has already hit, remember you just have to ride it out—but if you're noticing cues like major fidgets or whining, offering movement options can give those big feelings a way out. Punching a pillow, a fast run around the yard, or rocking together in the big chair—these simple physical actions can help your child's body process what their minds aren't yet equipped to handle.

And here's something else that's important to remember: as movement is an essential outlet for young children, not getting enough of it in a day can lead to a meltdown all by itself.

Change the temperature. When you're supporting an upset child, temperature interventions can be very effective. They create novel sensory input that interrupts a child's emotional storm, giving their overwhelmed system a concrete physical sensation to focus on and helping them find their way, eventually, back to a calmer state.

Cold can work wonders. Help your child splash cool water on their face or arms, or give them a cold drink with a straw—the combination of the cold sensation and sucking motion naturally activates calming signals throughout their body. Offer an ice pack to put over their eyes or a cool cloth for the back of their neck, or let them put their hands in a bowl of water with ice cubes in it. All of these options provide both a sensory reset and a distraction from their swirling emotional state. If it's cool outside, just stepping outdoors for a few minutes can help break through the distress (and don't forget nature has an inherently calming effect).

If warmth is called for, you could offer a heating pad, a hot water bottle wrapped in a towel, or a thick, cozy blanket to curl up in for a sense of security and physical comfort. In my house, we always had various sensory stuffed animals and weighted eye pillows around that we could put in the microwave and then snuggle up with. My kids would ask for warm "honey tea" during difficult moments (they believed it was some kind of magical calming tea, not learning until years later that it was literally hot water with honey in it). Just holding the warm mug in their little hands helped them calm themselves.

Sing or play soft music. Your child's brain responds differently to your voice than to anyone else's—they find it more comforting. When you sing to your child, it does something pretty remarkable: it reduces stress hormones in both of you, calming the whole situation down. Your singing actually slows your child's heartbeat and helps them breathe more steadily. It doesn't matter what it sounds like. Tap into your nurturing instincts; the sound of your voice is what they're responding to.

You could try singing a simple, calming phrase over and over, like "You are safe, it's OK." When my daughter was upset at night, I used to sing to a made-up melody: "Mommy loves you, and Daddy loves you, and Nana loves you too . . ." (It went on and on—please refer to page 156 for how she never slept—until I had sung the names of all our relatives, her stuffed animals, and the guy who came to fix the fridge that day.) She asked for it most nights; the repetitive, singsongy melody helped her focus and settle.

Playing slow, calming music at a certain tempo can feel very calming to your child as well. This isn't appropriate in all situations, but when you feel it might work, the right song can ease a child's distress by giving their nervous system a gentle, rhythmic structure to follow.

There's actually a specific tempo that works—sixty to eighty beats per minute—which helps soothe upset children because the tempo matches a relaxed heartbeat. A child's body naturally synchronizes with it; their rapid heart rate and quick breathing gradually slow down to match the music's rhythm. The predictable, consistent beat creates a sense of safety when children feel overwhelmed. Plus, the steady rhythm of music can help block out other noise and give children a simple focus point that holds their attention without being more stimulating, which is the last thing we need in a meltdown situation.

Here's a list of songs for you to try.

SOS Playlist

Get this calming playlist right here. These gentle, slow-tempo songs (all between sixty and eighty beats per minute) can help soothe and calm your child during moments of upset or distress.

1. "No More Worries"
2. "I Will Be Here"
3. "When You Sleep"
4. "Mama Nature"
5. "Just Be"
6. "Colors"
7. "I Have a Light"
8. "All Tucked In"
9. "On the Waves"
10. "How Do I Feel?"
11. "Sleepy Eyes"
12. "Peaceful and Calm"

Build a Foundation of Trust and Safety That Lasts

If you've ever felt completely unprepared when your child's emotions exploded, I get it. The truth is, no parent feels ready for these moments, but now you have something most of us didn't: actual tools that work.

The strategies in this chapter aren't abstract concepts—they're proven methods from real-life parenting experiences. When you stay anchored during your child's storm, validate their feelings instead of dismissing them, and listen with "What else?" instead of rushing to fix, you're teaching your child that big emotions are survivable, that they can count on you to stay steady no matter how big the waves get.

Your child won't remember every tantrum (though you might), but they will remember that you stayed calm, that you didn't abandon them when things got hard, and that your love wasn't conditional on their behavior. That's the foundation of emotional intelligence—and it creates lasting trust between you and your child.

When you use these Calm & Connect steps, you'll Create:

More of This

Staying relatively calm and grounded when chaos erupts

Connecting with your child before correcting them

Acknowledging your child's feelings, even when you disagree

Knowing it isn't about you

Trusting that the storm will pass

Giving yourself grace when you're in survival mode

Less of That

Joining your child in the emotional storm (co-escalating)

Trying to reason with an overwhelmed child

Getting frustrated when you can't stop the tantrum

Taking the tantrum personally

Expecting yourself to handle every crisis perfectly

Feeling embarrassed about public meltdowns

More Joyful Days Are Ahead: You Have Everything You Need

You now have something powerful in your hands: a road map for creating the joyful, connected family life you've been dreaming of. On the days when everything goes smoothly *and* on the days when it all falls apart, you now have practices that will strengthen your connection with your child—practices rooted in play, movement, and joy, the things that light kids up.

By honoring your child's natural way of being in the world, these tools tap into how they're designed to learn. Use them consistently, and you'll build a foundation that serves them for life. You're not just managing today's challenges more easily, you're raising a human being who will carry this capacity for calm, self-awareness, and mindful presence into their friendships, their work, and eventually their own families.

All the activities from this book—complete with videos, songs, and additional resources—are waiting for you at my website, where you can watch demonstrations, listen to the music, and discover even more ways to bring joyful connection into your daily life.

Remember, the key elements are already in place: your deep love for your child, your willingness to meet them where they are, and your commitment to showing up with presence. The rest is just practice. Trust the process, trust your child, and, most of all, trust yourself.

Acknowledgments

I'm incredibly grateful to everyone who helped bring *The Joyful Child* to life. It's quite a list. Here's my best shot at saying thanks, which feels a touch inadequate, but here we go.

THANK YOU:

To Suzie Barbour, my chief strategy officer, who walked alongside me through every stage of this process—guiding, supporting, brainstorming, and texting in all caps when necessary. To say I wouldn't be here without you is not overstating it. Your strategic genius, along with your genuine care for this work, has helped me build this platform and reach families around the world.

To Kris Carr, the first person who told me I should write a book (I think I laughed, sorry about that). You saw what I couldn't see yet. I'm grateful for the introductions that you made, which of course leads me to . . .

My agent, Stephanie Tade, who "got it" from day one and championed this project with passion and expertise. Thank you for sending me back to the drawing board to get the book proposal right, for helping me dig deep to articulate what I'm all about, and for believing in the power of this work for families.

To my editor, Marnie Cochran, who understood immediately that this book needed to feel like an easy chat with a trusted friend, and for letting it sound like me. Your guidance has made it infinitely better.

To Anni Betts, my incredible illustrator, who's provided the beautiful art for all my children's books and the cover art for this one. I cannot imagine any of my books without your gorgeous illustrations.

To Mandi Rivieccio, for your quiet brilliance and gentle nudging to see the big picture. To Abigail Ortiz, for your rock-solid support and unflappability—you make things easy for me and I'm grateful. To Justin Barbour, Cameron Brandt, and Bryce Scruggs for all the work behind the scenes that makes projects like this possible. To Richelle Fredson, for your expert guidance with my book proposal.

To my amazing Rockin' Yoga community members around the globe—educators, kids' yoga teachers, occupational therapists, dance instructors, and child-wellness professionals who share the vision of raising mindful, joyful children. Your expertise, stories, support, and enthusiasm have shaped me and my work in countless ways.

To the teachers, administrators, and school staff who have welcomed me into their classrooms and assemblies. Your dedication to children's well-being, often under incredibly challenging circumstances, is amazing.

To the thousands of children I've had the privilege to sing, dance, and breathe with in schools, libraries, yoga studios, community centers, and childcare facilities across the country and virtually all over the world—you taught me what truly works for you and what doesn't, and we've had so much fun along the way.

To my amazing collaborators who have helped shape my work—together we've played in bands, produced albums, pulled off all manner of events, taught unruly groups of children, and survived countless road trips. You've helped me find my voice and made me a better artist in every way: Katie Brennan, Dave Padrutt, Eve Sheldon, Kevin Soffera, Leo McClusky, Noah Jarrett, and Zak Rizvi.

To the teachers and community of River Valley Waldorf School, especially my children's wonderful early childhood teachers from whom I learned so much. You showed me what honoring childhood looks like—the profound beauty of protecting their wonder and letting them be children for as long as we can.

To Jen Sherman, Olivia Arena-Miller, and Jess Jacob, all incredible caregivers for my children when they were little. I'm so grateful for the gentleness and joy you brought into our home—all the kite flying, board games, watercolors, and pie baking were life-giving for me and for the kids. And somehow the house was always cleaner when I got home than when I left.

To Renell Carpenter, my carpool buddy/running partner/what's-for-dinner commiserator who has dissected every aspect of our collective five kids' development with me from lactation troubles to post-college angst. You took your girls to a little Waldorf school where the children played outside every day and sang and made art and did woodworking and knitted; I told you it was nuts to drive forty minutes each way to get there. Then I visited, and drove my kids there every day for the next fourteen years.

To my husband, David, and my big, wonderful family on all sides for cheering me on along this unconventional career path, and for never telling me to get a real job. Special shout-out to my big brother Tom, who's always believed in me and gives me the kicks in the butt I sometimes (OK, often) need. To my three children—Lola, Tristan, and Brody—thank you for letting your stories into the book. There are so many incredible ones from those funny, messy, joyful years when you were growing up, it was hard to choose.

To my Grandma Henry, who taught first grade since approximately the beginning of time (or that's how it felt when I was a kid in her house). How I wish we could sit at your kitchen table so I could tell you all about what I do now. It wasn't until recently that I realized something you used to say all the time—which kind of annoyed me when I was a teenager—has become the heart of what I believe about raising children, and the core message of this book: "It doesn't have to be so hard."

KIRA WILLEY is the author of seven bestselling children's books that have been translated into twenty-four languages, including the beloved number one bestseller *Breathe Like a Bear*. Kira is also a world-renowned recording artist, the co-creator and host of three PBS mindfulness, music, and yoga television programs, and the creator of Rockin' Yoga school programs. As a yoga teacher and lifelong musician, Kira's unique and powerful method of integrating music and movement into joyful, child-centered mindfulness practices has resulted in millions of streams, hundreds of thousands of children's book sales, and a massive, devoted fan base spanning the globe. A mother of three, she lives in Bethlehem, Pennsylvania.

kirawilley.com
Instagram: @kirawilley
Facebook.com/kirawilley
YouTube: @kira-willey